Stock Trading Tips
for beginners

Dana DeCecco

Former Commodity Trading Advisor and 15 year independent trader.

Dana has authored hundreds of published financial articles. His first book, "2 Trade Smart", covers the basic methods of technical analysis. He maintains websites dedicated to basic and advanced trading skills.

Lakeside21.com

DISCLAIMER

Trading futures, forex, stocks, and options involves the risk of loss. Please consider carefully whether futures, forex, stocks, or options are appropriate to your financial situation. Only risk capital should be used when trading. Investors could lose more than their original investment. You must review the customer account agreement prior to establishing an account. Past results are not indicative of future results. The risk of loss in trading can be substantial, carefully consider the inherent risks of such an investment in light of your financial condition. The author is not affiliated with any brokers, people, or companies mentioned. Opinions expressed by the author are by no means a solicitation of any kind.

Before trading options please read the publication "Characteristics and Risks of Standardized Options" available from your options broker.

DEDICATION

To Joseph
One Tough Hombre

CONTENTS

Acknolwledgements

FOR IMAGES AND CHARTS:

DAN DECECCO PHOTOGRAPHY
COMPARE BROKERS.COM
FREESTOCKCHARTS.COM
OPTIONSXPRESS
INVESTORS BUSINESS DAILY
BARCHART.COM
THE STREET.COM
BIGCHARTS.COM
SEASONALCHARTS.COM
CBOE
STOCK-ENCYCLOPEDIA.COM
SCHAEFFERS RESEARCH
NASDAQ
FINVIS.COM
ETF INVESTMENT OUTLOOK
INTERACTIVE BROKERS
DIVIDEND INVESTOR.COM
DIVIDEND.COM
YAHOO FINANCE
DIVIDATA.COM
BRAINYQUOTE.COM

Don't gamble; take all your savings and buy some good stock and hold it till it goes up, then sell it. If it don't go up, don't buy it.

Will Rogers

1 Online Trading

The number of self directed trading accounts have greatly increased due to the incredible access to markets and information. The home based trader can effectively compete with investment professionals.

Trading your own investment account online can be a rewarding endeavor. Learning a few simple trading methods can greatly increase your retirement income.

The methods described in this book are easy to learn and easy to implement. You can use some of them or all of them. Using only one of these techniques can enhance your bottom line by a significant amount.

This book is for the average investor that is tired of lousy returns on their investment capital. In recent years, many investors have watched their retirement accounts decline in value. The "buy and hold" days are long gone.

A few minutes each week is all you need to implement some of these trading strategies. The more time you invest, the more trading strategies you can use.

Online trading can be challenging and fun. It will take a little time to learn these methods but you only have to learn once. Soon they will become second nature and you will retain this knowledge for the rest of your life.

The first thing to do is to open an account with an online broker. There are many to choose from and you should do your homework before deciding.

Fees

	E*TRADE	optionsXPRESS	Ameritrade	Scottrade
Stocks Trading Fee	$9.99	$8.95	$9.99	$7
Options Trading Base Fee	$9.99	$0	$9.99	$7
Per Contract Options Fee	$.75	$1.25	$.75	$1.25

Here are a few listed above that I have used in the past. The cost per trade should not be a prime consideration unless you intend to become a very active trader. Open up a practice account and navigate through the site.

Select a broker that has a website you are comfortable using. Self directed trading should be fun, and not a chore. Online broker websites vary and often include services such as market news, charting software, and portfolio tracking.

OptionsXpress specializes in option trading and has great option chains. They also have very good option trading tools and good technical charting software. They offer extensive educational material and a practice trading site.

TDAmeritrade carries a wide variety of investment products. They have tools and platforms to suit any kind of investor. They offer education, research, and information on retirement accounts and goals.

Take your time and select a broker you like. You can also open multiple accounts with different brokers. Many brokers offer a sign-up bonus depending on the initial investment you plan to make. IRA accounts are available and there are incredible tax advantages for those trading from an IRA or Roth IRA. Benefits range from tax deferment to tax free. Check with your broker or tax consultant for more information about tax advantages.

You will have the option of opening a cash account or margin account. A margin account will enable you to leverage your investments. Your broker will lend you a portion of the capital required to buy shares. Trading on margin will magnify your profits and losses. If you are confident in your ability to trade wisely then open a margin account.

You also have the choice to enable your account for option trading. Options can be a great risk aversion tool and many of the tips in this book make use of option trading. The option trades covered in this book are not complicated. They are easy to understand and implement.

Option trading is not considered investing. Options are speculative in nature but if used correctly can enhance your investment tactics. Be sure to read "Characteristics ans Risks of Standardized Options", available from your broker.

This book is about earning a decent return on your investment capital. It is not about some get rich quick scheme. I will explain the upside and downside of the methods described. All of my clients have increased their annual return by applying only one or two of these trading ideas.

Most investors assume that their broker or account handler is a well informed expert at buying and selling stocks. Unfortunately, this is not the case. To think that an investor could lose half of the account value because of a market decline is ludicrous.

There is no "buy and hold" rule. You don't have to buy and hold anything. Did these guys ever hear of cash? What is wrong with exiting your trades and assuming a cash position?

I have heard so many horror stories about people losing half their retirement income. It just makes me sick. They have watched their hard earned savings dwindle away while their broker appears helpless to stop the bleeding. Investing should not be this way and you have the power to change it.

If you were competent enough to earn the money in the first place then you should be competent enough to invest it for a reasonable return. A reasonable return is not too much to ask for. Why would you pay someone to lose your money?

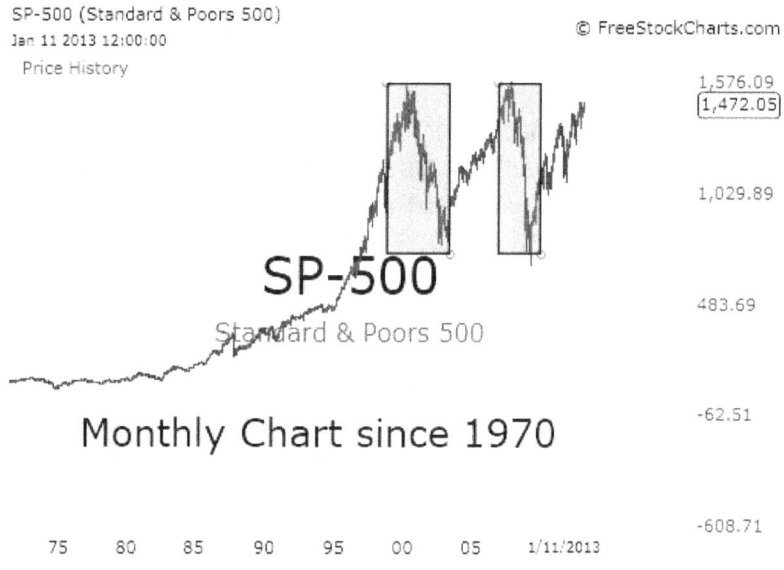

Only a fool would ride these waves. What is the point? You lose your money, you get it back, over and over. How about if you skip the part where you lose your money or at least cut your losses to an acceptable level.

4

The procedure is very simple. It will cost you some discount broker commissions and a little time. The net result will be an exponential increase in your annual return. It is well worth the effort.

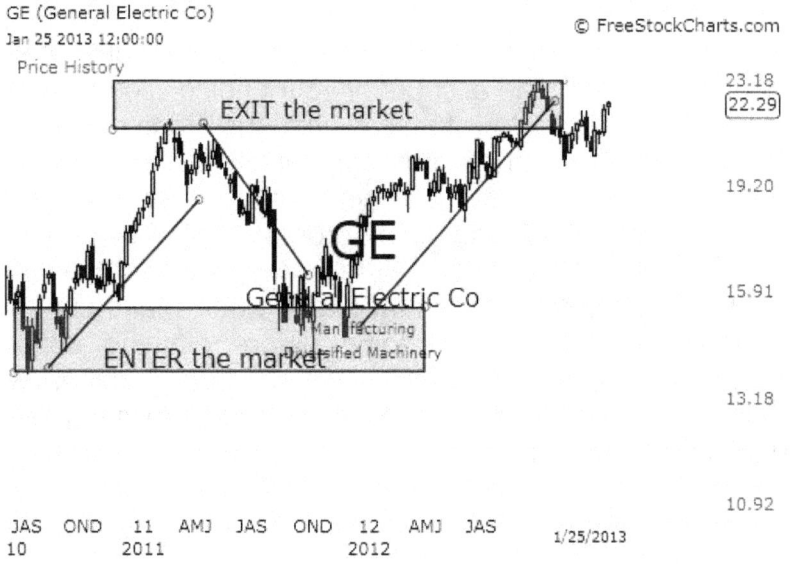

This isn't rocket science. Buy your stocks when they are cheap and sell them when they are expensive. Maintain a cash position during the market decline.

Many online brokers will pay interest on your trading account balance. Check with your broker before opening an account. You can make money on the way up and earn interest on the way down.

You don't need to be a market wizard to implement this simple strategy. You need to learn how to use your brokers trading platform and order entry system. You will also need a short course in how to read a price chart.

5

Even though the stock market is manipulated, you can still take measures to earn a descent return on your money. I cover market manipulation in my first book, "2 Trade Smart", which covers more advanced trading concepts. We will stick to very basic, simple, and easy to implement trading ideas in this book.

I will assume that you have selected your favorite online broker and opened the account of your choice. The next step is to become intimately familiar with the trading platform. This is where you actually buy and sell stocks. Most brokers have a practice version and you should use it to enter various types of stock and option orders.

You do not want to enter an incorrect order. Make sure you understand what you are doing before pushing buttons. Never, ever, be in a hurry to make a trade. Proceed with caution. Go slow and double-check everything. Patience is a virtue when investing your money.

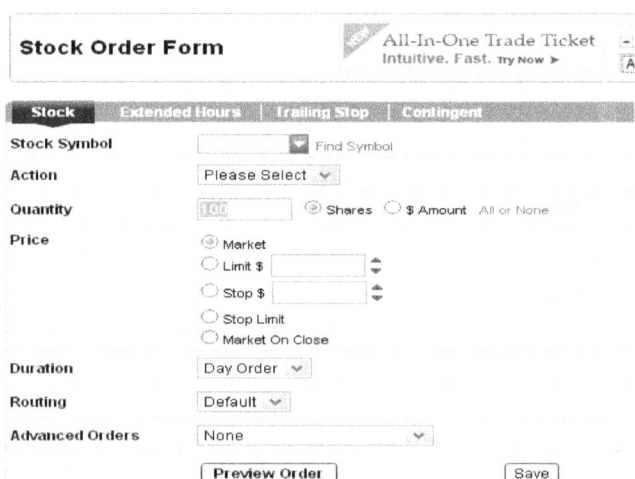

Notice the "Preview Order" button. This is a safety feature for novice traders. It allows you to double check your order, margin, available funds and order details before finalizing the trade.

I rarely enter a market order. During times of a fast moving market, your order may be filled at an undesirable price. I suggest using limit orders to make sure you get filled at a price you are willing to pay. If you don't get filled, so what! Good trading opportunities abound, there will be another one coming soon.

This brings up one of my RULES, "never marry a stock". I am not in love with any of these companies. In fact, I don't like any of them. I just trade them to make money. Companies fail for a variety of reasons. These days, international trade plays a big role in company failure.

Do you want to bet your retirement income on some management team? Not me. I don't trust them with my money. This brings up another RULE, "don't put all your eggs in one basket". Never allocate a large portion of your money to a single stock.

You can invest in a variety of stocks. Exchange Traded Funds (ETFs) are a great way to diversify your investments. They trade like stocks and don't carry the management fees of Mutual Funds. Many are optionable, which is advantageous, as you will find out later in this book.

There are two schools of thought on researching and analyzing stocks, fundamental and technical. Fundamental analysis is time consuming and is best performed by a service such as Investors Business Daily. They will rank and rate stocks according to fundamental values at a very reasonable cost to you.

They analyze thousands of stocks. It is not possible for the individual investor to do this. What a bargain!

The second type of analysis is technical. It is simply the ability to analyze price charts. I will cover the basics of this type of analysis and teach you enough to make educated decisions. I prefer technical analysis over fundamental because I think the truth is on the price chart.

Cooking the books seems to be an American pastime but due to our modern technology, cooking the price charts is also becoming popular. Diversification is one step in overcoming this problem. Chart reading methods can detect manipulation in many cases.

You can achieve a good return on your investment if you use the tools provided in the following chapters. Even if you only use one or two of these trading methods, you can greatly enhance your bottom line.

I am not going to delve into fundamental analysis since IBD and other services will do it for you cheaper than you can do it yourself. Just use the services to come up with the best fundamentally sound companies to trade.

Technical analysis, on the other hand, is something you should do yourself. Chart reading is a matter of interpretation and there are a number of variables. Barchart.com provides a free technical analysis service with buy and sell recommendations.

I think Barchart provides a great service but you can't beat evaluating the price charts yourself. You can use any combination of fundamental and technical analysis. Once you select a handful of your favorite stocks you will rely on fundamental analysis less and less.

You certainly don't need to analyze thousands of stocks on a regular basis. Your brain will explode because there is way too much information.

"If you do not read the newspaper, you are uninformed, and if you do read the newspaper, you are misinformed."
Mark Twain

Learn to read the charts. HISTORY IS ALL YOU GOT.

I use a program by Worden Brothers called Freestockcharts.com to sort stocks according to price, volume, beta, dividend yield and other factors. Even the free version is adequate for trading stocks.

Symbol	Volume ▾	Price	Beta	Dividend Yield
BAC Bank Of America Corp	145.9M	11.63	+1.78	+0.30%
SIRI Sirius Xm Radio	142.6M	3.16	+1.66	0.00%
NOK Nokia Corp Ads	129.3M	4.70	+1.76	+4.20%
RIMM Research In Motion Ltd	111.0M	13.56	+1.54	0.00%
FB Facebook, Inc.	89.6M	31.72	N/A	0.00%
F Ford Motor Co	67.6M	14.00	+1.51	+1.50%
S Sprint Nextel Corp	67.2M	5.92	+0.93	0.00%
MSFT Microsoft Corp	55.5M	26.83	+1.17	+3.40%
BBY Best Buy Co Inc	45.8M	14.21	+1.45	+5.60%
INTC Intel Corp	44.9M	22.00	+1.03	+4.30%
WFC Wells Fargo & Company	44.1M	35.10	+1.17	+2.50%

US Common Stocks ▾
Sort: Volume ▾   Desc Add Column

The paid version is jam packed with all kinds of sorting capabilities. TC2000 is my favorite stock analysis program and it is a bargain at less than $30 per month. It includes technical and fundamental aspects of analysis.

Selecting your analysis choice depends on how much time you intend to devote to your trading account. I think it is fun, so I devote lots of time. If you think it's a chore, just stick to the IBD picks and perform the simple charting that I will show you in the next chapter.

"One way to stop a runaway horse is to bet on him."
Jeffrey Bernard

2 Basic Charting

Basic charting is simple. You look at a price chart to determine if the stock is going up or down. Up is towards the ceiling and down is towards the floor. We can draw some lines on the chart to help us see it better.

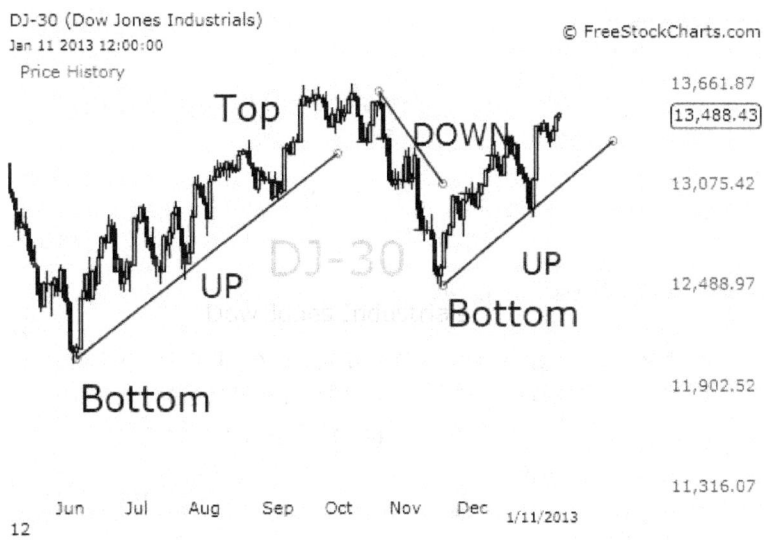

Stocks and all markets in general go up and down. This is a price chart of the Dow Jones 30. The price is listed in the vertical column on the right. The time line is listed in the horizontal row below the chart. The information available on this chart is price and time.

The price goes up and down over time forming tops and bottoms. The price is always going up, down, or consolidating in a sideways channel.

- We will never know where the exact top or bottom will be.
- We will never catch the maximum profit potential on every trade.
- We will always enter the market a little early or a little late.
- We will always exit the market a little early or a little late.
- There will always be money left on the table that we "could have made".

And, by the way.............

- There is nothing wrong with "not being in a trade" and maintaining a cash position.
- There is nothing wrong with getting out of a bad trade with a small loss.

And let us not forget..........

- If our trading is an emotional event just get out, quit, hire a manager, no sense reading this book.
- If we are not prepared to make a good trade, we will make no trade.
- We will only select the best of the best trading opportunities.
- We are never in a hurry to enter or exit any trade.
- We are never positively, absolutely sure about anything.
- We dislike all companies equally.
- We are just in the game to make money.

Anywhere in the shaded rectangle is a good time to buy Verizon because it is near a bottom. If the price continues down then we may have to hold the stock for a longer period of time. We will sell it when it gets near the top.

These charts were made on Freestockcharts.com, which is a free program for anyone to use. They offer charts on just about everything with all kinds of drawing tools. Try it out. It is very easy to use.

Most investors buy and sell stocks at the wrong time. Professional traders do the exact opposite. This is why you need to look at charts.....to see what is going on.

The "big money" traders do things to initiate a response from the average investor. GOOD NEWS can be leaked at the proper time to get investors to buy. BAD NEWS can be leaked at the proper time to get investors to sell.

The people reporting the news are clueless. I avoid news on individual stocks.

DJ-30 (Dow Jones Industrials)
Jan 11 2013 12:00:00
© FreeStockCharts.com
Price History
13,661.87
13,488.43
13,075.42
12,488.97
11,902.52
11,316.07

Investors buying
Pros selling

Investors selling
Pros buying

Investors selling
Pros buying

May 12   Jun   Jul   Aug   Sep   Oct   Nov   1/11/2013

Investors sell after they have lost enough money to run them out. Investors buy when times are good and the market is in a buying frenzy. Fear and greed are running the show. This reasoning is backwards, and the pros are counting on it.

Investors should be selling stock when the price is getting close to a top. A prime example is pictured in the shaded oval. Investors can simply sell their shares and assume a cash position.

Most investors won't sell at this point because they are greedy and want more profit. Greed will destroy you in the trading game. If you have made a reasonable profit then what is wrong with leaving some on the table? My attitude is better safe than sorry. You will never catch every bit of profit that is possible on a trade and neither do the professional traders. The pros know they can't have it all and move on with a reasonable profit.

14

Most investors will not buy when the market is down because of fear. Fear will destroy you in the trading game. There is nothing wrong with accepting a little risk to achieve a profit. In fact, assuming risk is the very nature of trading. If you are unwilling to assume risk, then get out of the market. There is no such thing as a risk free trade.

Fear and greed are forces that drive the market.

Most stocks track the market as a whole. If the market is rising, the stock is rising. The investor must follow the the big indexes such as the SP-500 or the DJ-30. You can draw lines where the price has changed direction in the past.

Price history holds clues to the future price action. History is the only indicator we have access to. The same rule applies to the super big trading syndicates. We have access to the same information as they do.

Program trading accounts for a large percentage of the daily trading volume. Computers are programmed by humans with access to the same information. They use price, time, and volume levels to create buy and sell signals.

Price, time, and volume are the only variables we have to work with. The hundreds of indicators you see on the charting platform are a variation of price, time, and volume.

There is nothing else.

The only advantage the big traders have is the ability to manipulate the market. Fundamental manipulation is accomplished using news, announcements, and special reports. Technical manipulation is accomplished by spending loads of money to create a chart pattern or market maker price adjustments.

Technical manipulation can be an asset to a technical trader. They need markets to go up and down so they can buy and sell at the right times to create profit.

The points where price has changed direction in the past is where we draw lines for future reference. The lines are called SUPPORT and RESISTANCE lines. These lines are the most important indicator for the chart reader.

The price on this chart has approached a resistance line. When the price is approaching a resistance line we should refer to our price charts more frequently to see if the price is going to change direction. This is NOT a good time to buy stocks.

If you are just getting into the market at this time you're just going to have to wait if you are a buyer. You might consider buying assets that are not correlated to the stock market. Some commodity ETFs such as GLD, which is a gold tracking ETF, may be a better choice. When the market is declining they may be advancing. Look at the chart.

The Street Ratings

10 Best Precious Metals & Gold ETFs
Top-Rated ETFs

RSS Feed for 10 Best Precious Metals & Gold ETFs for 2013

Top Precious Metals ETFs as of 11/30/12

Fund Name	Get Info
ProShares Ultra Gold	UGL
ETFS Physical Swiss Gold Shares	SGOL
SPDR Gold Shares	GLD
iShares Silver Trust	SLV
PowerShares DB Silver Fund	DBS
PowerShares DB Precious Metals Fund	DBP
PowerShares DB Gold Fund	DGL
UBS E-TRACS S&P 500 Gold Hedged	SPGH
ETFS Physical Palladium Shares	PALL
PowerShares DB Gold Double Lg ETN	DGP

GLD (SPDR Gold Trust)
Jan 11 2013 12:00:00
© FreeStockCharts.com

Buy assets when they are near a bottom. Do not buy assets when they are near a top. Although we can not know exactly where the top or bottom may be, we can certainly see the difference between high and low. Stocks are high and gold is low. Buy low and sell high. This one simple method will give you an edge in the marketplace.

Just like going to the grocery store, we are looking for a bargain.

17

This stock is not bargain priced. Even though the price may continue to rise, the odds are against it. We want the odds on our side.

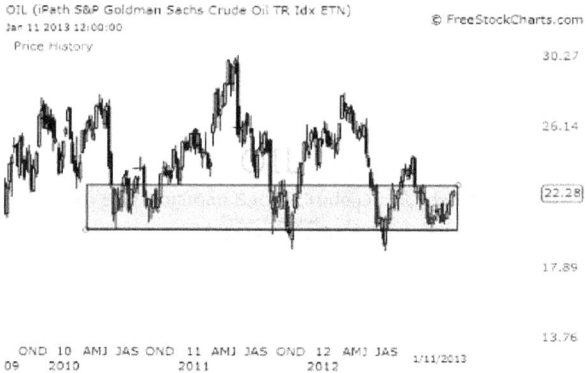

Now this oil ETF looks like a bargain because the price is near the bottom. The price may continue to decline but the odds are against declining past the lower support line. This would certainly be a better choice than the Home Depot stock above.

Some price charts are easy to read and some are difficult. Why bother trying to analyze a difficult price chart when there are thousands to choose from? Just move on.

At any given time there are many good trading opportunities to choose from. If you can't find one, don't trade.

18

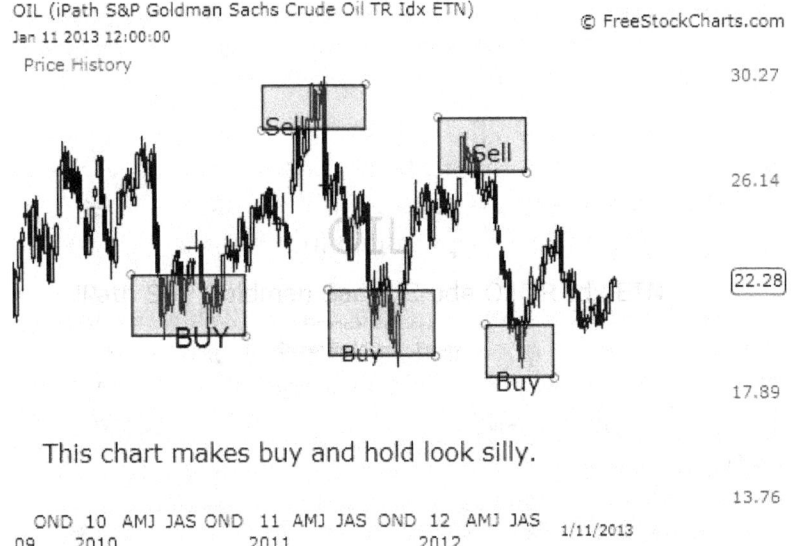

OIL (iPath S&P Goldman Sachs Crude Oil TR Idx ETN)
Jan 11 2013 12:00:00

© FreeStockCharts.com

Price History

30.27

Sell

Sell

26.14

22.28

BUY

Buy

Buy

17.89

This chart makes buy and hold look silly.

13.76

OND 10 AMJ JAS OND 11 AMJ JAS OND 12 AMJ JAS 1/11/2013
09   2010   2011   2012

A buy and hold strategy on this oil ETF would have resulted in little, if any, profit for the investor. Buying at the bottoms and selling at the tops would have resulted in a very profitable trade for the investor.

Selling your shares at the tops will adjust your account to a cash position. Just wait until the price hits bottom to buy it again. Do this over and over again.

Buying at the top and selling at the bottom is not an exact science. We don't know exactly where the top or bottom is going to be or when it is going to happen. The more proficient you become at reading the charts, the closer you will be able to estimate tops and bottoms. You will rarely catch the full price increase or eliminate the full price decrease.

We are trying to capture as much of the up-move as possible. We are trying to eliminate as much of the down-move as possible. We are NOT buying at the top and selling at the bottom.

19

Technical analysis is a big subject and is covered more fully in my first book. I just want to cover a few basics for beginners here. Up to this point we have learned:

- Stock prices go up and down
- Tops and bottoms are pivot points
- Pivot points create support and resistance lines
- These lines can be probable future turning points

This may seem over-simplified but few investors will follow these principles. It goes against our human nature to buy something that has failed or lost value. We want to buy a successful company and that is why most investors buy at the top.

Nobody wants a loser, so investors sell the failing stock at the bottom just before they lose all their money. The crowd behaves opposite to the professional traders. It's just human nature.

I am going to cover one more technical analysis tool in this chapter. Moving averages are easy to implement on the price chart and can be very useful. I use the 200, 50, and 20 period simple moving average settings. You can set this up on any charting platform.

A large percentage of the professional trading is called program trading. Computers are programmed to enter and exit trades at predefined signals. One of these signals is moving averages.

You can install the moving average on your chart under the indicators tab. MA is short for "moving average" and SMA is short for "simple moving average". Just enter the period. The "period" is simply the time frame of the chart you are viewing. The "daily" time frame and "weekly" time frame are the most important charts for casual investors.

You can install as many moving average studies on the same chart as you like.

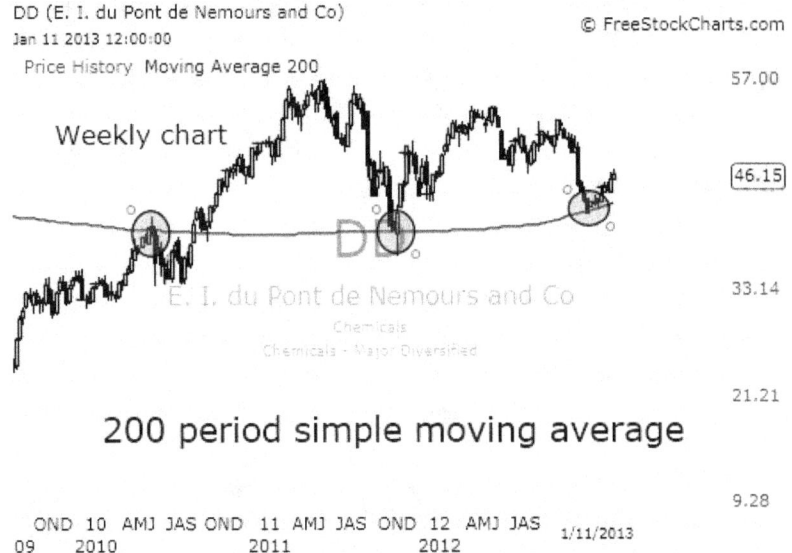

DD (E. I. du Pont de Nemours and Co)
Jan 11 2013 12:00:00
© FreeStockCharts.com
Price History Moving Average 200

Weekly chart

57.00

46.15

33.14

21.21

200 period simple moving average

9.28

OND 10 AMJ JAS OND 11 AMJ JAS OND 12 AMJ JAS 1/11/2013
09 2010   2011   2012

Notice on the chart above how the price bounces off the moving average. This is not always the case. The moving average is either working for a particular stock or it is not. It is working if it is being used by the program traders.

All indicators are subject to whether they are being used. Any indicator may work for one stock and not for another. You can easily tell by looking at the chart and see if it is working. If it has been working in the past, there is no reason to believe it will not continue to work. If it fails, stop using it.

In the following chart CSX is bouncing off the 200 period simple moving average. Maybe Warren Buffet buys this railroad when the price touches the 200 period SMA. Who knows? And further more, who cares. We are not concerned why it works.

We are only concerned if it works.

We would expect this stock to once again bounce off the moving average and advance. The odds favor this happening. The Las Vegas book makers would put the odds in favor of a price increase. We are just playing the odds, and we want them in our favor. Odds are calculated on historical evidence.

Daily Price Chart

34.96

31.51

28.03

24.54

21.06

lay   Jun   Jul   Aug   Sep   Oct   Nov   Dec   1/14/2013
12

20 day SMA, simple moving average

This is a great chart for a swing trader. This type of trading has a time horizon of a few days to a few weeks.

Weekly Price Chart

36.29

32.99

29.24

22.19

15.13

8.08

OND 10 AMJ JAS OND 11 AMJ JAS OND 12 AMJ JAS   1/14/2013   JAS
09 2010   2011   2012

50 week SMA, simple moving average

This weekly chart is more suited to a longer term investor. Each trade will last for months. The time frame you select will depend on your personality and circumstances. I am too impatient for long term investing and I think day trading is too stressful. I swing trade the daily, four hour, and one hour charts.

You don't need to be an expert chart reader to increase your returns. Most people ,that I have taught, use very little of the methods that I have just presented. Their average rate of return is better than 15% annual. They do not spend much time trading and are very happy with the returns they are getting.

You decide how much time you want to put in and how much money you want to make. I am putting the information out there. Use what you want and disregard the rest.

If you take the initial time to develop a good investment system, fear and greed will have no effect on your bottom line. Learn the basics once and just do the same thing over and over. Eliminate stress and get a reasonable return on your investment.

"There are two kinds of investors, be they large or small: those who don't know where the market is headed, and those who don't know that they don't know. Then again, there is a third type of investor -the investment professional, who indeed knows that he or she doesn't know, but whose livelihood depends upon appearing to know."
Bernstein, William.

Draw support and resistance lines near the area you are trading. Far away lines are of no value to us now.

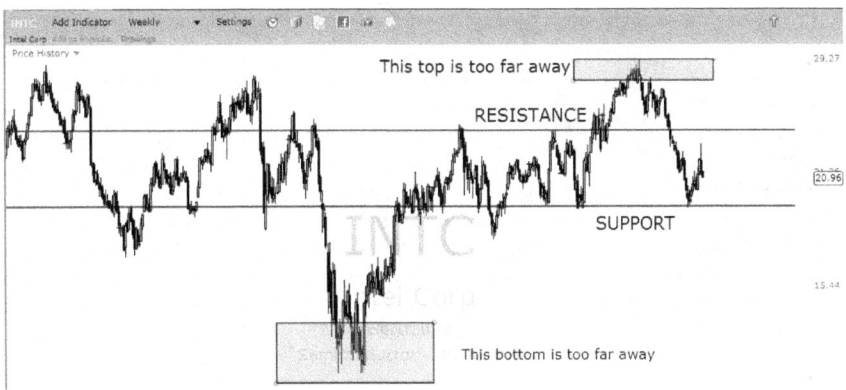

The price on this chart of INTC is right in the middle of support and resistance. This does not give us any indication of future price direction.

There is no trade here. Move on to the next chart. You may have heard the GREAT NEWS about Intel. You can trade it if you want. But I gave you fair warning about the news.

Price charts have many points of support and resistance. We are only concerned with the ones nearest to the current price.

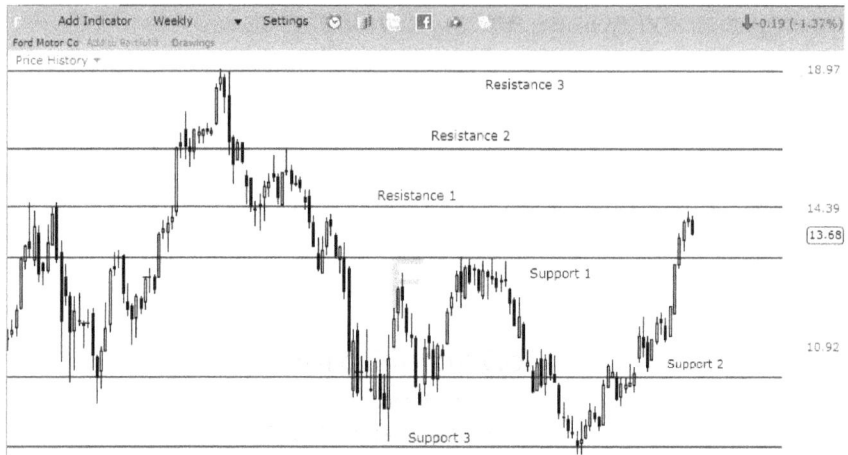

In this price chart Ford is bouncing off resistance. This is a great time to sell Ford and a bad time to buy Ford.

I personally ignore the news about individual stocks. I follow the major market news with a skeptical attitude.

I believe what I see on the historical price chart. If I enter a short position (sell) Ford at this time , the price may break up past the resistance line. Bad trades are part of the game.

I would exit the trade with a small loss and move on to the next trade.

... when you have eliminated the impossible, whatever remains, however improbable, must be the truth.

Sir Arthur Conan Doyle

3 Get Creative

Most novice investors are unfamiliar or unwilling to enter a short position. Shorting a stock is selling a stock that you do not own. Your broker will lend you the stock so that you can sell it, but sooner or later you will pay back the loan.

I consider this trade to be too risky for novice investors. The potential for loss is unlimited. You can accomplish the same trade using options. Option trading is not necessarily risky or complicated.

Options can be used as insurance policies for shareholders and limited risk trades for speculators. You can buy them and sell them.

There are two types of options, CALLS and PUTS. For now, we will focus on BUYING calls and puts.

- Buying a put gives you the right to sell the stock, at the strike price you select, on or before expiration.
- Buying a call gives you the right to buy the stock,at the strike price you select, on or before expiration.

Option contracts are for 100 shares of the underlying stock. These contracts expire on the third Friday of each contract month. You can buy the contract in the month you select. I always allow enough time for the price to move the desired amount.

Let's try a "protective put" example:

You bought 100 shares of INTC for $19.50. INTC is currently priced at $22.00 so you are up $2.50 per share or $250. You don't want to sell because you think there may be more upside profit to be made but the general market is due for a correction.

The following chart indicates that the SP-500 may be due for a correction since it is bouncing off a resistance line.

Since most stocks follow the market in general, INTC will

most likely take a down turn with the market. So what choices do you have?

- Hold the position, take the loss and recover
- Sell the stock, buy it back when it is lower
- Hold the position, buy a protective put
- Sell the stock, buy a speculative put

The first choice is the "buy and hold" scenario. The second choice we have already covered in a previous chapter. The last two choices are option trades.

Price charts will show you how long it usually takes for the price to move a substantial amount. There is no reason to think it will be different in the future. It may be different in the future but:

Ya gots to work with what you gots to work with.
Stevie Wonder

Well said, little Stevie. We work with historical evidence and the evidence favors a market correction.

- An aggressive trader may initiate a trade based on the information provided so far.

- A conservative trader may wait for the SP-500 price chart to retreat a little more before making a decision.

I am generally in the conservative camp. I require more confirmation before making a decision. There are no absolutes in trading.

To trade options you need to learn to read the option chains. The option chains are where you can find the:
- expiration months
- strike prices
- option prices (or premiums)
- and a whole lot of other stuff that does not need to be covered in this book

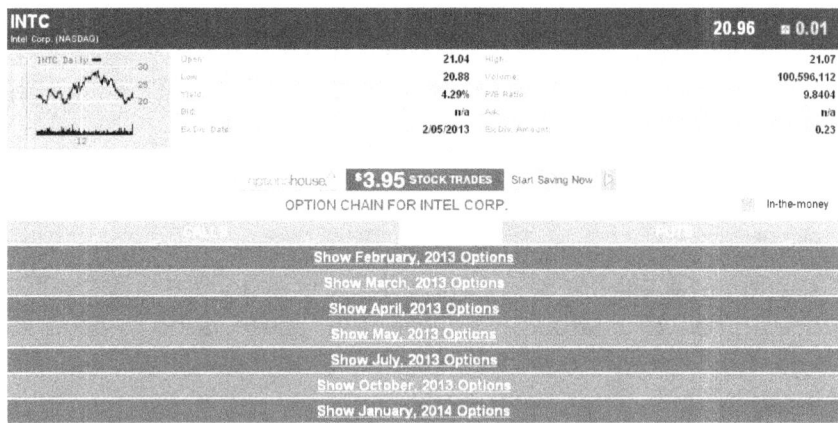

This is the front page of the option chains from BigCharts.com. The first action is to select the expiration month. Leave enough time for the price to move.

If you choose to hold your position, keep the stock, buy a protective put. Go to your brokers option chains. There you will find the different contract months, strike prices and premiums.

Strike	quote	0.07		167.00	Premium	
20.00	quote	0.14	-0.03	4,501	0.14	0.16
21.00	quote	0.36	0.01	2,201	0.35	0.36
21.93						
22.00	quote	0.79	-0.02	3,312	0.79	0.81
23.00	quote	1.49	-0.02	953.00	1.49	1.50
24.00	quote	2.35	0.03	183.00	2.36	2.38
25.00	quote	3.30	-0.05	150.00	3.30	3.35

From our example, INTC is currently at $22 per share. The $22 PUT is priced at 0.81 or $81 per contract. This particular contract expires in six weeks.

For the next 6 weeks you have the right to sell INTC for $22 per share, in effect, insuring your profit. If INTC tanks to $15 per share, instruct your broker to exercise your contract and your shares will be sold for $22.

If INTC moves up to $24 per share you can sell back whatever value is left on your put contract. If you wait until expiration, the contract will expire worthless.

Since this book is about stock trading tips I am not going to provide detailed education about option trading. I will introduce you to the possibilities using options and allow to to pursue your option education.

Another possibility is to sell your stock at the current value and open a short option position. A short option position is simply buying a put. As the value of the stock decreases, the value of your put will increase.

Refer to the previous option chain. The $22 put option was selling for .081

The price of INTC has dropped and the value of the $22 put option will increase.

20.00	quote	0.15	0.08	9,353	0.14	0.16
21.00	quote	0.45	0.26	17,678	0.44	0.46
21.25						
22.00	quote	1.09	0.76	10,097	1.07	1.11
23.00	quote	2.00	1.15	1,559	1.99	2.01
24.00	quote	3.13	1.33	177.00	2.98	3.05

The put option has increased from .081 to 1.07 as a result in the decline in price. This is an easy way to profit during downward price moves. Closing your option position is selling it back at the increased value. It is a simple procedure.

Put options can be used to:
- Insure your existing position
- Speculate on downward price moves

Either way, you can profit from adverse price moves. You don't have to hold your position and watch your money disappear. Learn to use options.

Adverse price movements happen on a regular basis. You don't have to ride the wave. You can, at least, get out of the market and assume a cash position. That is better than losing money.

If you take the time to learn basic option trading, you can profit from market downturns.

" A stock broker is one who invests other people's money until
its all gone."
-Woody Allen

Buying and selling calls and puts is easy to learn and relatively safe. Your maximum loss is limited to the premium (or price) you paid for the option. When you close your long option position, the cash is immediately credited to your account.

We have learned the value of buying puts, but what about calls. You would buy a call to open a long position on the underlying stock. You think the price will go up. You can buy a call instead of buying the stock. It requires less investment capital and the maximum loss is the premium paid for the option.

The downside of buying a call is the time limit of the option. Timing your trade is the key to earning profits. Your purchased option loses time value every day.

You are not required to hold your option position for any length of time. You can sell it back anytime for the remaining value. If your trade is going bad, you can bail out and recover a portion of your loss.

The value of a long call will increase as the price of the underlying stock increases. One ATM long call will go up in value approximately fifty cents for each one dollar increase in the underlying value of the stock.

If the trade progresses as planned, you have the choice of closing your option trade for cash or exercising the option and convert it to actual ownership of the shares. Of course, you will be required to put up the margin for the stock purchase.

The call option gives you the right to buy the shares at the strike price on or before expiration. Lets say you bought a call on Ford.

Ford has gone up about $3 since you bought the call. If you purchased the $10 strike price, then you have the right to buy Ford shares at $10 per share. You can exercise your option and own 100 shares of Ford worth $1,400 for $1,000. If you think Ford may head south, you can sell the stock and collect your profit.

You can play this up and down game with the same stocks over and over. It is best to limit your "universe of stocks" to a handful. There is no need to search the entire market each time you want to place a trade.

If you become familiar with a few stocks, you will begin to understand how they move under certain market pressures. Pick stocks that seem to move up and down on a regular basis. These are called "Rolling Stocks".

Trading a handful of your favorite stocks will give you an edge over the investor always searching for a new stock to trade. Trading a few stocks will simplify your fundamental analysis. Your technical analysis charts can be saved and used over and over again with the support and resistance lines already on them.

Select the stocks you can afford to trade. 100 shares of a $10 stock will cost you about $500 on margin. 100 shares of a $70 stock will cost you $3,500 on margin.

Try to trade in lots of 100 shares. Odd lot shares are harder to sell and option contracts are in lots of 100 shares.

Avoid trading stocks with an average daily volume of less than 200,000 shares. This is the absolute minimum. Over one million shares daily is best.

Biotech stocks can be risky. Any business that must rely on the Federal Government to approve their product could be a disaster waiting to happen. On the other side of the coin, you could get rich quick.

Many stocks exhibit seasonal tendencies. Retail stocks generally appreciate prior to the Christmas holiday season. Seasonality is generally attributed to the commodities market. Many companies are correlated to commodities in one way or another. For example, gold mining stocks generally track the price of the commodity GOLD.

| Home | Spot | Futures | Volatility | Cycles | Intraday | Weather | Indices |
| Start | FAQ | Info | Strategies | | Seasonality | | |

Explanation about Seasonality

- Causes of seasonal trends
- Non-seasonal price movements
- Single years
- The stability of seasonal trends

SeasonalCharts.com could give you a "heads up" on your next stock trade.

All markets are correlated or non-correlated in some way.

" There are three classes of people who don't think markets work: the Cubans, the North Koreans and the active fund managers."
Rex Sinquefield

4 Simple Option Trades

There are two other simple option plays that will increase your profits. These are both option selling(or writing) methods that your account must be enabled for. Brokers provide option levels according to account size and experience. You can request an upgrade at any time.

October. This is one of the peculiarly dangerous months to speculate in stocks. Other dangerous months are July, January, September, April, November, May, March, June, December, August and February.
Mark Twain

Our first option strategy is called selling(or writing) cash secured puts. Selling a PUT is a strategy used to collect the premium and also used as a means of acquiring the underlying stock for less money.

The stock selected should be a stock the investor is willing to purchase. This strategy is best implemented if you intend to buy the stock anyhow.

The stock should be poised for an increase in value which means it is near a bottom. Technical analysis of the chart pattern should indicate the stock price is likely to increase.

Writing a put requires an _obligation_ on the part of the trader. The put writer is _required_ to purchase the number of shares contracted at the strike price selected, on or before contract expiration.

 The put writer collects a premium for the sale of the option contract. As long as the price of the underlying stock remains above the strike price, the option will not be exercised by the buyer. The put writer will retain the premium paid, and have no obligation to purchase the underlying stock.

If the stock declines in value, the trader faces the possibility that the stock will be _put to him_. The put buyer is exercising his option. In this case the put seller will be required to purchase the stock at the strike price selected.

The put seller will retain the premium paid for the sale. This scenario will result in the trader buying the stock at a discount to the selling price of the stock at the time the position was entered.

Although the objective is to collect the premium without having the stock PUT to them, it may be desirable to buy the stock if it is low enough in price. This may result in a longer term trade. The put writer may have to hold the stock until it appreciates in value to make the trade profitable.

The PUT writer wants the underlying stock price to rise. If so, the stock does not have to be purchased. The premium can be kept in either case. The stock may be a desirable purchase at this price and will be purchased if it declines (drops under the strike price).

Upon selling the option, this premium is deposited into the investors account. The seller of a PUT is required to have the cash equivalent of the margin needed in reserve, the broker will put a hold on the funds needed for the purchase.

Each brokerage firm may have different requirements on the cash needed for security. The use of margin will increases the risk / reward of each trade.

Using this strategy you either get the stock at a discount price or get paid for NOT buying the stock. This trade is as close as it gets to a risk free trade.

Let me repeat that. The result of using this strategy is:
- A) You will be required to purchase the stock at a discount price. OR
- B) You have been paid for not buying the stock.

By now, you should be reading the last two pages again, a little more carefully.

Let's take an example.

Consolidating near a bottom

MSFT has been consolidating near the bottom for weeks and is due for a breakout. You are willing to pay $27.25 per share for the stock. 100 shares will cost $2,725 and you will have to put up about $1,350 in margin to buy it.

Why pay the asking price if you can get it at a discount price?

Why not get paid to NOT buy MSFT?

Let's check out the option chain to see what kind of deal we can make.

25.00	quote	0.24	0.01	179.00	0.22	0.24
26.00	quote	0.45		581.00	0.44	0.45
27.00	quote	0.82	0.01	440.00	0.82	0.83
27.25						
28.00	quote	1.41	0.05	534.00	1.41	1.43
29.00	quote	2.19	-0.01	216.00	2.19	2.21

If you are willing to pay $27 per share, your broker will pay you $82. The broker will hold the $1,350 margin during the trade which could last up to 2 months.

The premium of $82 is a 6% return on your investment of $1,350. You could make this trade 6 times in one year which would give you a 36% return on your investment.

So what is the downside? If the stock drops below $27 per share it may be put to you. You will have to buy it for $27 per share. But wait. You have already been paid .82 per share so you are actually paying $26.18 per share. This is a savings of $1.07 per share.

If you are confident that MSFT will quickly rise above $28.00 per share, your broker will pay you $141 NOT to buy MSFT. Refer to the option chain above. That is a 10.4% return on your money but the stock is more likely to be put to you. You might have to pay $28 per share less the $1.41 received or $26.59 per share. This is still a $.66 savings per share.

So why would you ever pay full price for a stock if you can buy it at a discount or get paid for not buying the stock?

Selling puts is my favorite stock trading strategy. If you are going to buy a stock anyhow, why not use this technique to get the stock at a reduced price.

The only downside to this strategy is that it will tie up your capital until expiration.

" Risk is good. Not properly managing your risk is a dangerous leap" -Evel Knievel

Lets try one more example.

Yamana Gold is sitting dead on support and you expect a rally in the price of gold. The current price is $16.29 so the margin for the trade will be approximately $800.

15.00	0.26	0	0.26	0.28
16.00	0.58	0	0.59	0.61
17.00	1.18	0	1.14	1.17
18.00	0.86	0	1.89	1.93

The $16 put is priced at .59 which is $59 per contract. That is a 7.4% return on the margin held. Expiration is 6 weeks off.

If you sell the put, the cash will be deposited to your account and the necessary margin will be put on hold. By selling the put you have obligated yourself to buy the stock for $16 per share on or before expiration.

At expiration if the stock price is below $16, you will be required to buy the stock. $16 less the .59 you were paid leaves you with a purchase price of $15.41.

If the stock price is above $16, you simply keep the $59 premium and allow the option to expire. That's it.

CBOE EXECUTE SUCCESS™

Who Should Consider Selling Cash-Secured Puts?

▶ An investor who would like to acquire shares in a particular security, but is willing to wait for them to trade at a target price that is below current market level

Have you ever entered a limit order to buy a security at a price below its current trading level? If so, you've most likely experienced a waiting game, and possibly a lengthy one because the stock will not be purchased until it trades at or below your limit price. Instead of simply waiting for that to happen you could take an approach that is a little more pro-active and sell (write) a cash-secured put. You will be paid, in the form of the premium received for selling the put, in return for accepting the obligation to buy underlying shares if assigned, and at a price lower price that you select in advance. Many large portfolio managers as well as individual investors find this an attractive means to acquire stock for their portfolios.

Check out the CBOE for more information.

The next simple option trade is selling covered calls. You will be selling a call option which is covered by your long stock position.

Call selling obligates the writer to sell the stock at the strike price on or before expiration. The bottom line here is that you can get paid for not selling your stock or you will have to sell it at a profit. Twist my arm.

Using the same MSFT example:

Consolidating near a bottom

Let's say the put selling trade did not work out and MSFT was put to us. We ended up paying $26.18 per share and the price is still consolidating near support.

If you are willing to sell it for $27 or $28 per share, you can check out the possibility of writing a covered call. Any option enabled account can make this trade because the risk is secured by ownership of the stock.

This trade can increase our return on investment if we are willing to sell the stock with a modest profit.

2.34	2.37	1,928	25.00
1.51	1.53	9,829	26.00
0.87	0.88	12,562	27.00
			27.25
0.43	0.45	19,591	28.00
0.20	0.21	24,099	29.00

We paid $26.18 for the stock. If we sell at $28 per share it will give us a profit of $1.82 per share. Not too shabby. That's a 13.8 % return on our investment of $1,350 margin.

But wait. Our broker is willing to pay us $.43 per share to sell our shares for $28. That would give us a profit of $2.25 per share or a 16.6% return on our investment.

If the price of MSFT stays below the strike price of $28 then we will simply keep the $43 and the trade is over. We still own 100 shares of MSFT and we can do it again and again and again.

If the price of MSFT goes above the $28 strike price, we will be forced to sell it for profit of 16.6%

So what is the downside of these trades? The company you are buying could go bankrupt or some systemic event could cause the market to crash. Every investor assumes these risks regardless of the technique used.

 Risk is part of the investing game.

" Sometimes your best investments are the ones you don't make." -Donald Trump

5 Orders and Risk

Novice traders can incur losses because they don't know exactly how to make the trade. Orders can be confusing. Much of this chapter is taken from another of my books but I think it's too important to omit in this book.

<u>Basic terms we use:</u>

When you BUY a stock, you are <u>opening</u> a LONG position (you think it will go up)
When you SELL(short) a stock, you are <u>opening</u> a SHORT position (you think it will go down)

When you BUY a stock that you have sold SHORT, you are <u>closing</u> a short position.(cover)
When you SELL a stock that you own, you are <u>closing</u> a long position.

No matter what trade you make, you are OPENING a position or CLOSING a position.
(other than adding to or subtracting from an existing position)

You can open a position LONG or SHORT.
You can close an open position.

These basic terms apply to stocks and options.

" Everyone has the brainpower to follow the stock market. If you made it through fifth-grade math, you can do it." -Peter Lynch

Basic Orders you need to know

MARKET order (buy or sell it RIGHT NOW , I don't care what price it is.)

LIMIT order (buy or sell it as soon as possible, at $XXX or better)
You tell them what you are willing to pay or what you are willing to sell for.
This type of order may not get FILLED , the price must remain beyond your limit until the order is filled.

STOP order (when the price hits $XXX, turn my order into a MARKET ORDER.

STOP LIMIT order (when the price hits $XXX, turn my order into a LIMIT ORDER.

A DAY ORDER is good for the day. This order will either be FILLED or canceled at the end of the trading day.

A GOOD TILL CANCELED order will either be FILLED or remain valid until you cancel it.

These are all the BASIC ORDERS you need to know. There are other types of orders for advanced players. You don't need them to trade profitably.

A good broker will fill your order AT or BETTER than what you asked for.

Order what you want

this is what you want:
XYZ stock has been coming down for weeks and is currently trading at $10 . You think its a good deal, but you don't want to pay more than $10 for it. It doesn't matter if you get filled today, as long as you get it for $10 or less.

You want to open a long position for 100 shares at $10 or less as soon as possible.

this is what you order:
Stock ticker: XYZ
Amt: 100
Type of order: BUY LIMIT
Limit price: $10
Good till Canceled

---

this is what you want:
Same as above, only $10 or so is close enough, and you want it right now.

this is what you order:
Type of order: BUY MARKET
Day Order

---

this is what you want:
Same as above,only you think it will go lower. You wont pay more than $9 for it. But its now or never.

this is what you order:
Type of order: BUY STOP LIMIT
Stop Limit Price: $9
Day Order

this is what you want:
Same as above, only $9 or so is close enough and there aint no hurry.

this is what you order:
Type of order: BUY STOP
Stop price: $9
Good till Canceled

THE MORE STRICT YOUR ORDER - THE LESS CHANCE IT WILL BE FILLED.

Order what you need

You own 100 shares of XYZ stock. You paid $10 per share. You want to sell it.
You want to SELL TO CLOSE your position.

This is what you need:
Your stock is currently trading at $15. You want out right now for around a $5 profit.

this is what you order:
Type of order: SELL MARKET
Amt: 100
Day Order

_____

this is what you need:
Your stock is trading at $15, but you think it will go to $16 and you will not sell for less than $16. No big hurry.

this is what you order:
Type of order: SELL STOP LIMIT
Stop Limit price: $16
Good till canceled

this is what you need:
Your stock is trading at $15. You have placed a sell stop limit to sell at $16. The market is volatile and the price may drop back to $10. You want to make at least $3 per share on this trade, more or less, and you want to protect this profit if the price drops.

this is what you order:
Type of order: SELL STOP (also referred to as a STOP LOSS)
Sell Stop price: $13
Good till Canceled

YOU ARE NOT CHARGED FOR AN ORDER UNLESS THE ORDER IS EXECUTED.

Just in case orders

this is what you want:
You have been watching XYZ stock for awhile. You don't have time to watch the market during the week. It's trading at $10 and you are willing to pay $8 or less.

this is what you order:
Ticker: XYZ
Amt: 100
Type of order: BUY STOP LIMIT
Buy Stop Price: $8
Good till Canceled

---

this is what you want:
You own XYZ stock. You paid $10. You don't have time to watch the market, but just in case the market spikes up to $15, you'll take it. Anywhere near that price is a great profit.

this is what you order:
Ticker:XYZ
Amt:100
Type of order: SELL STOP
Sell stop price: $15
Good till Canceled

Make sure your broker is using the same terminology that I am using here. Some brokers differ slightly. DONT MAKE A TRADE UNLESS YOU KNOW WHAT YOU ARE DOING.

You can issue as many orders as you like as long as your account is funded well enough to cover them.

I hope that I have provided enough examples. These combinations can go on and on. Your orders depend on your circumstances and what you are trying to accomplish.

order ticket

Stock	Extended Hours	Trailing Stop	Contingent

Stock Symbol	AKS Find Symbol
Action	Buy
Quantity	100 ⦿ Shares ○ $ Amount All or None ☐
Price	○ Market ○ Limit $ 13.50 ○ Stop $ 13.50 ⦿ Stop Limit ○ Market On Close
Duration	Good Until Cancelled
Routing	Default
Advanced Orders	None

Preview Order   Save

Risk Management

Yes, your money is at risk if you have an open position in the market.

Do not trade without a Money Management Plan and a Trade Management Plan. Always keep in mind that if some terrible event occurs, such as 911, the entire market could crash and you may lose ALL of your money. This is called SYSTEMIC RISK, and it is the risk that every participant in the market assumes, whether they want to or not.

Well, that's the bad news. The good news is that you can control the amount of non-systemic risk that you are willing to assume.

RISK and REWARD go hand in hand. The more risk you are willing to assume, the more profit or loss you will take. This is just common sense. However , there are skills that you can learn that will lower your risk.

If we utilize a money management plan and place our trades carefully, we may be able to tip the scales in our favor.

A money management plan is very easy to set up. It is based on HOW MUCH WE CAN LOSE. Everyone wants to know how much they can make. Well, the answer is THE SKY IS THE LIMIT.
If I ask you how much you can lose, the answer will not be THE SKY IS THE LIMIT. This is exactly the question you should be asking yourself. How much am I willing to lose?

This is why we are constantly preaching DO NOT TRADE WITH MONEY YOU CANT AFFORD TO LOSE. If you want to gamble, go to Vegas. It's more fun than trading.

The easiest way for me to explain how to set up your money management plan is by example.

Let's say that you have a $2000 trading account for trading stocks. You are just learning to trade and you are prepared for some losses(even the best pro's have losses).

With $2000 , you want to open a MARGIN account. You will have to come up with half the cost of a stock purchase. Your broker will lend you the rest. This will allow you to look at stocks priced up to $20 per share or so. So now, your universe of stocks may be SP-500 stocks priced under $20.

The question is how much can you trade for and how much can you lose on each trade.

My general rule is "risk no more than 5% of the account value on each trade" so we will use this for our example. 5% of $2000 is $100. So we can't lose more than $100 per trade.

Larger account sizes should have a lower risk per trade such as 2% or 3%

You decide to buy 100 shares of AK Steel @ $15 per share. You need to place a STOP LOSS order at $14 per share. $1 times 100 shares = $100 loss. That is a pretty tight stop loss unless AKS is sitting on a major SUPPORT line.

Maybe it would be better to buy Dryships. DRYS is trading at $5 per share. We need to place our SELL STOP at $4. This is a wide stop, and gives us plenty of breathing room. If DRYS is sitting on SUPPORT we may decide to place our STOP LOSS at $4.50, giving us a $50 loss if the trade goes bad.

The general idea here is to know how much you can lose BEFORE entering a trade. If you are willing to lose 10% of your account value on each trade, then adjust the formula accordingly.

Combine your money management with the laws of support and resistance. And here is a tip: don't place your stop too close to the support line. The Market Makers may drop the price just below the line to TAKE OUT the trades before running the price up.

These examples are based on the assumption that you are not a long term buy and hold investor. If you are buying stocks to hold and collect dividends, a stop loss order may not be appropriate.

Most stocks will eventually turn profitable sooner or later. The market has been going up since 1920. The 2 exceptions are the tech bubble of 2000 and 911. These are systemic events and the risk involved is known as systemic risk. Stop loss orders are appropriate for swing traders and other short term traders.

I don't know how much money you can make trading the markets. If you do not know how to place an order, you will lose money. If you do not manage your risk, you will lose money. If you can learn the lessons I have given you so far, you just might make some money trading.

The following advise is for investors interested in developing a more concrete trading system. The casual investor may not be interested in devoting more time to trading. You do not need to know this information unless you intend to advance your trading efforts.

All trading systems must have three basic components. These components are Money Management, Risk Management, and Trading Rules. Many trading accounts have been wiped out due to a poor or even no money management plan.

Many novice traders concern themselves with how much money they can make when they should be concerned with how much money they can lose. To begin with, the trading account itself should be comprised of risk capital. Beyond that, an acceptable loss per trade must be determined.

A good rule of thumb may be 3% to 5% of total account value for a reasonable loss per trade. For example, with an account size of $2000, an acceptable loss per trade would be 5% or $100. With a maximum loss per trade of $100 we can now determine which securities or options we are able to trade.

We could purchase an option contract for $100 or less. We could also trade a modestly priced stock. The money management plan can be applied to any market. Just do the math.

The next component of the trading system is Risk Management. Part of the risk management plan has already been determined. We will lose a maximum of $100 per trade.

There are two ways to accomplish this. The first is to sit in front of the computer and watch the screen as the trade develops with your finger on the exit button. The other, and much easier on the nerves way, is to initiate a stop loss when the position is opened.

This "set it and forget it" method takes all the emotion off the table. The only reason to watch a trade progress is to manage an early exit to cut losses or profits. If you have developed a sound system, there is no need to cut out early.

The third component of the trading system is the actual trading rules. Systems can be automated or manual, in other words you can visibly see the trade signals develop on the chart or you can set up a software program to do it for you. You can even purchase one from me at fxharmonic.com.

It is best for the novice investor to manually trade the system. Our beginner system is buying near the bottom and selling near the top. This is as simple as it gets but I will explain a little more advanced concepts.

Most trading systems have been developed through the use of back testing or forward testing over a period of time. A system can be based on price action, indicators, and chart patterns.

Your system will need an entry signal and two exit signals. One exit will be for a profitable trade and the other exit will be for a losing trade. The exit strategy must be formulated before entering the trade. The profit potential and maximum loss must be set before entering the trade.

After extensive testing has been done, you should have a probability of wins and losses which can be stated in a ratio such as 1/2 meaning one out of two trades is a winner. You should also have a Risk/Reward or profit and loss ratio such as 1/2 meaning the system will risk one dollar to make two dollars.

Then you put it all together and you may have a system that wins two dollars and loses one dollar 50% of the time. If you can develop a system such as this you will be a wealthy trader in no time at all. The point is, before trading, work the numbers. Know how much you can win and how much you can lose.

" 90 % of the people in the stock market, professionals and amateurs alike, simply haven't done enough homework,"
-William J.O'Neil

6 Exchange Traded Funds

Exchange Traded Funds are called ETFs for short. ETFs are traded exactly like stocks. They can be analyzed through charting methods and many have options available.

There are different kinds of ETFs. They are designed to track various securities such as:

- Indexes
- Industries
- Bonds
- Currencies
- Commodities

This opens up a very wide range of assets for the average investor. ETFs help to mitigate risk because you are not investing in a single company with a single management team. Broad based investing spreads the risk over a larger portion of the market.

All of the trading methods we have learned so far apply equally to trading ETFs. Keep in mind that when selecting stocks and ETFs the average daily trading volume should be at least 200,000 shares. Anything less could result in liquidity problems.

A liquidity problem could result in a delay selling your asset. Technically, there must be a buyer for each seller. Most brokers will let you slide on this and buy your shares, but I wouldn't bet the farm on it.

Symbol	Volume	Price	Beta	Dividend Yield
SPY SPDRs S&P 500 Trust S	169.5M	148.33	+0.99	+2.80%
XLF SPDRs Select Sector Fir	56.9M	17.15	+1.26	+2.40%
EEM iShares MSCI Emerging	51.7M	44.78	+1.35	+0.10%
EWJ iShares MSCI Japan Ind	48.7M	9.86	+0.68	+2.00%
VXX iPath S&P 500 VIX Shor	45.5M	23.98	-5.00	0.00%
QQQ PowerShares QQQTrust	32.0M	67.07	+1.09	+2.20%
IWM iShares Russell 2000 In	23.2M	88.57	+1.27	+3.30%
FXI iShares FTSE/Xinhua Ch	20.0M	41.70	+1.10	+0.40%
EFA iShares MSCI EAFE Inde	18.8M	58.15	+1.21	+2.10%
IYR iShares Dow Jones US F	17.3M	67.38	+0.97	+4.80%
UVXY	17.0M	11.56	N/A	0.00%

US Exchange Traded Funds ▼
Sort: Volume ▼   Desc   Add Column

Freestockcharts.com provides a scanning and sorting service for stocks and ETFs. Pictured above are some of the most heavily traded ETFs. Many ETFs pay dividends.

Notice the BETA column in the image. Beta is the measure of the percentage of movement compared to the total market index (SP-500). SPY moves almost exactly with the market.

A beta greater than 1 means the security is more volatile and less than 1 would be less volatile. A simple way to look at it would be to say that if SPY goes up $1 then the FXI will go up $1.27 because the beta is +1.27.

Some assets have a negative beta. This means that they move opposite to the market. If the market is going up, they are going down. If the market is near a top, they are near a bottom. Beta should be used as a "rule of thumb" and not be used to calculate exact trade parameters.

Many novice traders can't seem to get it in their head that you can make a profit when the market is going down. I guess it must be human nature. Negative beta ETFs may help to solve this problem. The SPY tracks the movement of the SP-500.

When the market appears to be nearing a top, just enter a long position on the reverse ETF. You can also use these ETFs to initiate our long option trades.

This is SPXU which is the opposite of SPY. When the market is moving down you can go long on this ETF.

You can use this ETF to apply our covered call and cash secured put strategies. The option chain is in increments of one dollar which makes it very convenient.

3.70	3.80	21.00	**30.00**	quote	0.45	0.20	357.00	0.40	0.55
3.00	3.20	183.00	**31.00**	quote	0.75	0.10	5.00	0.80	0.90
2.45	2.60	181.00	**32.00**	quote	1.20	-0.10	42.00	1.25	1.35
2.05	2.15	121.00	**33.00**	quote	1.70	0.15	1.00	1.80	1.95
			33.33						
1.70	1.80	75.00	**34.00**	quote	2.40	-0.05	61.00	2.45	2.55
1.40	1.50	172.00	**35.00**	quote	3.10	0.30	1.00	3.10	3.30
1.15	1.25	378.00	**36.00**	quote	3.80	0.52	10.00	3.90	4.10
1.00	1.10	1,127	**37.00**	quote	2.20	-1.15	5.00	4.50	4.90
0.80	0.90	158.00	**38.00**	quote	5.00	-0.02	20.00	5.50	5.70
0.70	0.80	97.00	**39.00**	quote	5.78	1.98	8.00	6.20	6.70

So now you can profit from a long position whether the market is going up or down. If you look at enough charts, you will see that the markets go down more quickly than they go up.

SPY (SPDRs S&P 500 Trust Series ETF)
Jan 18 2013 12:00:00
© FreeStockCharts.com
Price History
158.73
148.33
125.57
92.41
59.25
26.09

Markets tend to FALL DOWN and CLIMB UP

08   09   10   11   12   1/18/2013

The down moves are much sharper than the up moves. You can make more money faster playing the market down. Fear may be a more powerful force than greed.

SPXU (ProShares UltraPro Short S&P500)
Jan 18 2013 12:00:00

© FreeStockCharts.com

Price History

60.62

50.73

40.85

33.33
30.97

The inverse ETF JUMPS UP and CLIMBS DOWN

21.08

lar   Apr May Jun Jul Aug Sep Oct Nov Dec 1/18/2013   Mar
12

Stock-Encyclopedia.com sorts ETFs according to general categories. Their top 100 list is sorted accorded to trading volume. ETFs offer products for a variety of assets.

Stock-Encyclopedia.com
ETF Guide

All ETFs

Category: All ETFs

Subcategories:

Stock ETFs   Bond ETFs   Commodity ETFs

Asset Allocation ETFs   Market Indexes   ETFs Listed on Global Stock Exchanges

A list of option enabled ETFs is available from Schaeffers Research.

ETF Master List

ETF Ticker	ETF Description	Sector	Optionable?	Tools
IBB	ISHARES NASDAQ BIOTECHNLGY	Biotechnology	Yes	Quote | News | Charts Option Chain
IEF	ISHARES TRUST	Bond	Yes	Quote | News | Charts Option Chain
LQD	ISHARES GS $ INVESTOP CP BD FD	Bond	Yes	Quote | News | Charts Option Chain
SHY	ISHARES LEHMAN 1-3 YR TREA BD	Bond	Yes	Quote | News | Charts Option Chain
TLT	ISHARES LEHMAN 20+YR TREA BD	Bond	Yes	Quote | News | Charts Option Chain
TTH	TELECOM HOLDRS TR	Communications	Yes	Quote | News | Charts Option Chain
VOX	VANGUARD TELECOMM SVCS ETF	Communications	Yes	Quote | News | Charts Option Chain
PBS	POWERSHARES DYN MEDIA PORT	Communications	Yes	Quote | News | Charts Option Chain
BDH	MERRILL LYNCH BROADBND HOLDR	Communications	Yes	Quote | News | Charts Option Chain
IYK	ISHARES DJ US CNSMR GD SEC IDX	Consumer	Yes	Quote | News | Charts Option Chain
IYC	ISHARES DJ US CNSMR SVC SECT I	Consumer	Yes	Quote | News | Charts Option Chain
XLP	SPDR FD CONSUMER STAPLES	Consumer	Yes	Quote | News | Charts Option Chain

The CBOE (Chicago Board Options Exchange) provides exhaustive information about ETPs. Exchange Traded Products is another name for ETFs.

Welcome to CBOE.com: the definitive source for options trading information.

CBOE is the world's largest options exchange and the leader in product innovation, options education and trading volume.

You may also run into the terms ETC and ETN. This is natural tendency for the "powers that be" to keep everyone in a state of confusion. They are all pretty much the same thing but read the specs before you invest.

Institutional investors move large sums of money from one sector or industry to another. This is called sector rotation. To keep tabs on where the money is coming from or going to, you can use heat maps.

Nasdaq provides a dynamic ETF heat map along with other market maps.

ETF Dynamic Heatmap®

Explore our NASDAQ-100 Heatmap and our NASDAQ-100 Pre-Market Heatn

View the price of 100 Exchange Traded Funds at a glance. Each colored rec

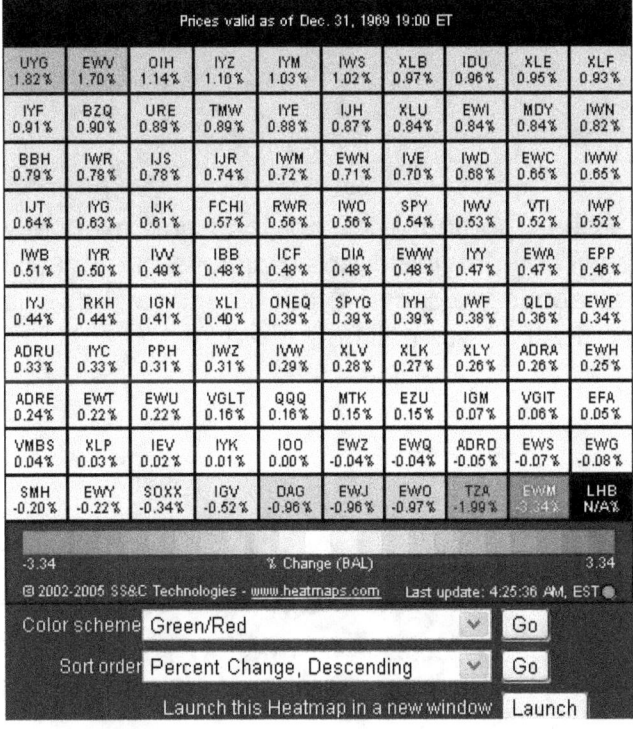

Before selecting a trade from the heat map, pull up a chart and visually analyze the price structure of the ETF. Is it near a bottom with money pouring in? Is it near a top with big money moving away?

Barchart.com is one of the best services for analysis. Most of their services are free. Barchart provides more information than you can use.

By Weighted Alpha ☑ HELP

Weighted Alpha	Industry Name	Change	Stocks	Links
+175.00	Top 100 Stocks	+1.12	100	📊 📈 📰
+88.60	Finance - Mortgage & Rel Svs	-0.69	7	📊 📈 📰
+75.45	Building - Residential & Comm	+4.77	17	📊 📈 📰
+73.60	Building - CMT & CNT & AG	-0.96	8	📊 📈 📰
+63.32	Building & Construction - Misc	+1.01	20	📊 📈 📰
+61.01	Building Prds Retail - Wsale	+1.40	9	📊 📈 📰
+54.73	Insurance - Life	+2.38	19	📊 📈 📰
+51.28	Building Products - Wood	+0.67	9	📊 📈 📰
+49.24	Medical - Hospitals	-9.74	11	📊 📈 📰
+48.42	Paint & Related Products	-0.51	4	📊 📈 📰
+47.06	Tools - Hand Held	-1.04	5	📊 📈 📰
+47.02	Building - Heavy Construction	-1.15	13	📊 📈 📰
+45.82	Building Prdcts - Air Heating	-0.64	5	📊 📈 📰
+43.75	Retail - Jewelry	+1.25	4	📊 📈 📰

This is a short portion of a very long and exhaustive list of industries. They provide charts, opinions and analysis. From the image above we can see that big money has entered the building industry. Let's pull up a chart.

MG631 (Residential Construction)
Jan 23 2013 12:00:00
© FreeStockCharts.com

Price History

851.35

635.09

462.81

337.26

245.77

Volume   Moving Average 20

25.0M
5.8M

JAS   OND   11   AMJ   JAS   OND   12   AMJ   JAS
10   2011   2012   1/23/2013

This chart is telling me that the Residential Construction industry has been rising for quite some time and may be near a top. Personally, I would not buy any stock or ETF related to this industry at this time.

Always pull up a chart and look at the big picture. The price on the chart above is very high and the volume seems to be fading away. This is not a good time to buy this industry.

Alpha is a measure of performance on a risk adjusted basis but this particular industry has already performed. This is not to say that the upward move is over. There is no absolute top. The absolute bottom is zero but the absolute top of any asset is undefined.

We can never know the top. We can only use historical evidence to provide a probable exit point for the big money. We are not looking for where the money has been. We are looking for where the money is going.

This is best accomplished by charting price action over time. If we are looking to buy an EFT then we are looking for an industry near a bottom.

Metals and mining look good at this time. Gold related assets often move inversely to the stock market.

Finvis.com provides great visual aids. This black and white book does not do it justice. Check it out online.

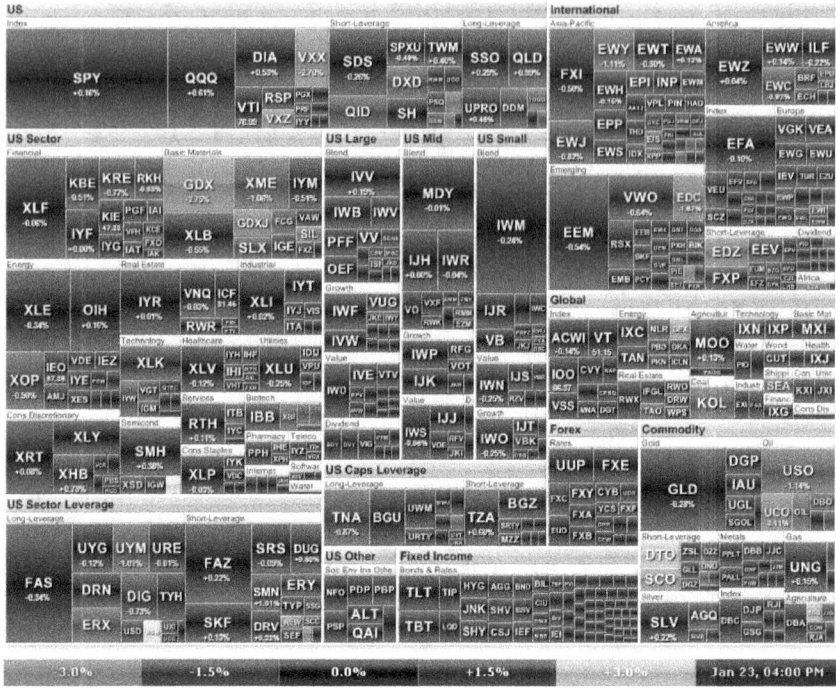

These are ETFs arranged by sector. Sectors are a group of related industries.

Sector rotation is very important when trading ETFs. The economic cycle keeps the economy healthy. The money keeps moving around and around.

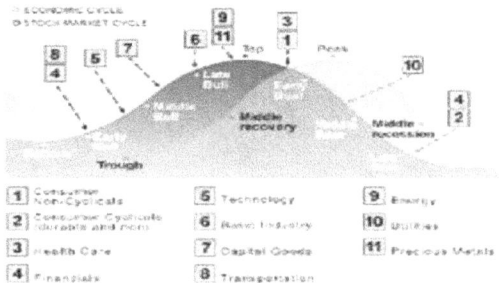

ETF investment outlook offers information and analysis.

ETF Investment Outlook

Home | Contact Us | About |

Commentary

Technical Talk

ETF Basics

ETF Rankings

Price Breadth

Volume Breadth

High-Low Breadth

McClellan Breadth

McClellan Volume

ETF Charts

by Category

by Family

Most Active

RSS

+ MY YAHOO!

MY AOL

+ Google

Bloglines

newsgator

Welcome to *ETF Investment Outlook*. This site features bro
McClellan Oscillator, the McClellan Summation Index, the I

* Last updated after market close on Wednesday, January 23, 2013

Top 10 - Advance-Decline Net% (all)

Name	Symbol	ADNet
Home Construction DJUS iShares	ITB	51.9%
Media PS DY	PBS	37.9%
Homebuilders SPDR	XHB	28.6%
Software GS iShares	IGV	28.3%
Semiconductors PS DY	PSI	23.3%
Retail HOLDRS	RTH	20.0%
Software PS DY	PSJ	18.5%
Networking PS DY	PXQ	17.2%
Oil Service HOLDRS	OIH	12.0%
Semiconductor HOLDRS	SMH	12.0%

Bottom 10 - Advance-Decline Net% (all)

Name	Symbol	ADNet
Gold Miners MV	GDX	-89.7%
Biotech HOLDRS	BBH	-84.0%
Banking PS DY	PJB	-80.0%
Oil & Gas Explor & Prod DJUS iShares	IEO	-63.9%
Biotech & Genome PS DY	PBE	-63.3%
Broker-Dealers DJUS iShares	IAI	-60.9%
Biotechnology SPDR	XBI	-60.9%
Regional Bank HOLDRS	RKH	-60.0%
Steel MV	SLX	-57.7%
Utilities SPDR	XLU	-54.8%

Online service providers offer more information than you can digest. Select your favorite few and keep it as simple as possible.

This gold related ETF is moving inversely to the SP-500.

Options are available on this ETF. Let's try a cash secured put example. The current price of GDX is $41.92. The margin required to purchase 100 shares would be approximately $2,100.

40.00	quote	0.84	0.28	3,689	0.84	0.84
40.50	quote	1.00	0.46	426.00	0.99	1.04
41.00	quote	1.19	0.39	1,744	1.18	1.19
41.50	quote	1.33	0.40	2,345	1.38	1.40
41.92						
42.00	quote	1.62	0.51	1,543	1.62	1.63
42.50	quote	1.90	0.61	648.00	1.89	1.90
43.00	quote	2.10	0.53	556.00	2.16	2.18

The premium on the $41.50 put is $1.38. Selling one put contract would pay us $138. This contract expires in six weeks.

This is a 6.6% return on our margin investment.

We also ave the option of initiating a covered call or buy/write.

3.25	-1.00	31.00	3.10	3.20	41.00	**39.50**
2.90	-0.80	153.00	2.78	2.82	710.00	**40.00**
2.54	-3.66	2.00	2.45	2.49	72.00	**40.50**
2.17	-0.81	99.00	2.14	2.19	303.00	**41.00**
1.97	-2.08	39.00	1.85	1.90	59.00	**41.50**
					Stock Price »	**41.92**
1.70	-0.63	771.00	1.59	1.64	261.00	**42.00**
1.45	-0.71	151.00	1.36	1.40	185.00	**42.50**
1.16	-0.60	395.00	1.14	1.18	6,941	**43.00**
1.00	-0.54	77.00	0.96	1.01	367.00	**43.50**
0.88	-0.41	275.00	0.81	0.83	1,489	**44.00**

This is a portion of the call option chain. If we buy 100 shares of GDX at $41.92 per share on margin it will cost us $2,100.

We can sell the $43 strike price for $114. This obligates us to sell our shares for $43 per share.

The $41.92 we are paying less the $1.14 we are receiving gives us an adjusted share price of $40.78.

If we get "called out" our profit will be the $43 sale price less the $40.78 purchase price or $2.22 per share. That's a 10% profit in six weeks.

If the price closes below the $43 strike price we will simply keep the shares and the premium for a 5.4% profit.

At this point we can hold the shares until the price increases and continue to sell calls.

" The problem with the person who thinks he's a long-term investor and impervious to short-term gyrations is that the emotion of fear and pain will eventually make him sell badly."
-Robert Wibbelsmen

7 Dividends

Dividend paying stocks and ETFs can provide a less volatile investment strategy. A number of factors should be taken into consideration before jumping in. The primary consideration in selecting a stock is the dividend yield.

The dividend yield compares the price per share to the dividend paid per share. The resulting number is a percentage of income to investment.

For example, if the price per share is $20 and the annual dividend is $1 the dividend yield would be 1 /20 or 5%. The higher the dividend yield, the more bang you're getting for your buck.

Buying dividend paying stocks on margin may not be a good idea. The interest paid for margin can eat away the dividend profits. Paying cash for these stocks may be the best plan. Margin rates vary greatly between brokers.

	$25K	$200K	$1.5M	$3.5M
E-Trade	7.94%	6.14%	3.89%	3.89%
Fidelity	7.575%	6.575%	3.750%	3.750%
Interactive Brokers[3]	1.63%	1.38%	1.00%	0.77%
optionsXpress	8.25%	7.00%	6.00%	6.00%
Schwab	8.00%	6.875%	6.25%	6.00%
TD Ameritrade	8.50%	7.25%	6.25%	6.25%
thinkorswim	8.50%	7.25%	6.25%	6.25%

Exhibit 1. Margin rates as of May 1, 2012. Source: Interactive Active Brokers website.

Rates also vary with account size.

Broker	Margin Rate (lowest to highest)
Interactive Brokers	1.570%
optionsXpress	6.250%
Zecco	7.750%
E*TRADE	8.140%
Fidelity	8.575%
TD Ameritrade	9.000%

Large accounts receive preferred rates from most brokers.

Margin rates are shown based on a margin balance range between **$10000.00** and **$19999.99**:

Broker	Margin Rate (lowest to highest)
Interactive Brokers	1.570%
OptionsHouse	4.000%
eOption	5.000%
Just2Trade	5.250%
optionsXpress	6.250%
SogoTrade	6.500%
ShareBuilder	7.200%
Scottrade	7.500%
Zecco	7.500%
Firstrade	7.750%
TradeKing	7.750%
Vanguard	7.750%
Fidelity	8.075%
E*TRADE	8.140%

A dividend paying stock purchased on margin and held for a year can actually lose money.

Interactive Brokers is obviously the best choice for margin traders. Their fees and commissions are also the lowest among brokers. The IB trading platform is fast and efficient but requires a learning curve and could be considered unfriendly to amateur investors.

Most trading platforms incorporate safety features such as previewing your order. This service helps novice traders to double-check their orders before entry. The IB platform is unforgiving but is my favorite platform as a professional trader.

If you are willing to spend the time learning the platform then Interactive Brokers can save you fees, commissions, and margin rates. The minimum deposit required is $10,000.

Make everything as simple as possible, but not simpler.
Albert Einstein

The majority of companies pay dividends quarterly. To collect a dividend you must own the stock before the ex-dividend date. These dates are published. There is no rule about how long you must own the shares.

The ex-dividend date is the last day for purchasing shares in the company to capture the actual dividend. The dividend may be released a few days later on the record date. Stock trades generally take a few days to settle or post on the books. The share owner on the record date will receive the dividend.

The stock price is usually lowered by the amount of the dividend on the day after the record date. So it doesn't pay to hold the stock for a few days just to collect the dividend.

It may be a good plan to buy the stock during an uptrend to capture the capital gain with the dividend being an added bonus. This method would capture the best of both worlds. We can utilize all the methods we have previously learned using dividend paying stocks.

The Street.com provides an ex-dividend calendar.

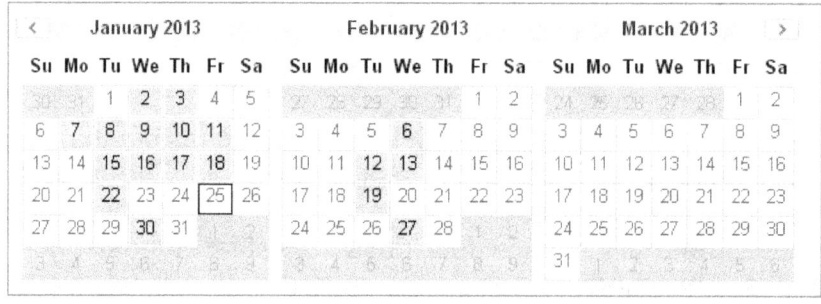

Just click on the date to see which companies you can buy to collect the dividend. Select a few candidates and then pull up a price chart to see if it is a good time to buy this company. Timing is everything in the investment game.

The goal is to capture both the dividend and the gain in stock value. There is no point in collecting the dividend and losing money on the trade.

Many investors just buy and hold dividend paying stocks at any particular time. With a little effort you can make money on both ends. Just use the same stock buying techniques we have learned in previous chapters.

<	January 2013						February 2013						March 2013						>
Su	Mo	Tu	We	Th	Fr	Sa	Su	Mo	Tu	We	Th	Fr	Sa	Su	Mo	Tu	We	Th	Fr	Sa

January 2013
Su	Mo	Tu	We	Th	Fr	Sa
	1	2	3	4	5
6	7	8	9	10	11	12
13	14	15	16	17	18	19
20	21	22	23	24	25	26
27	28	29	30	31		

February 2013
Su	Mo	Tu	We	Th	Fr	Sa
					1	2
3	4	5	6	7	8	9
10	11	12	13	14	15	16
17	18	19	20	21	22	23
24	25	26	27	28		

March 2013
Su	Mo	Tu	We	Th	Fr	Sa
					1	2
3	4	5	6	7	8	9
10	11	12	13	14	15	16
17	18	19	20	21	22	23
24	25	26	27	28	29	30
31						

Symbols for 01/18/2013

Symbol	Company	Amount	Yield	Dividend ExDate
CLX	Clorox Company	$0.64	3.39%	01/18/2013
LOW	Lowe's Companies Inc.	$0.16	1.80%	01/18/2013

You can pull up a quick chart on Yahoo Finance which also provide dividend information or use Freestockcharts.com for an interactive chart.

In the above example I have clicked on the January 18 box and two stocks post the ex-dividend date, Lowes and Clorox. The amount of the quarterly dividend is posted along with the yield.

Before buying any stock we will pull up a price chart and get a visual analysis of the big picture. We don't want to buy a stock just to collect the dividend. We are looking for a stock poised for a price increase.

The ex-dividend date is in the shaded oval. The date of record was 2 days later. This could be a good trade for a very short term trader but I would avoid this trade. The dividend does not justify buying this stock at the already high price of $77.17. Most investors are looking for a longer time horizon.

The monthly price chart reveals that CLX is at an all time high. Always check out the larger time frames.

The Dividend Investor will provide more information than you need for a reasonable monthly fee.

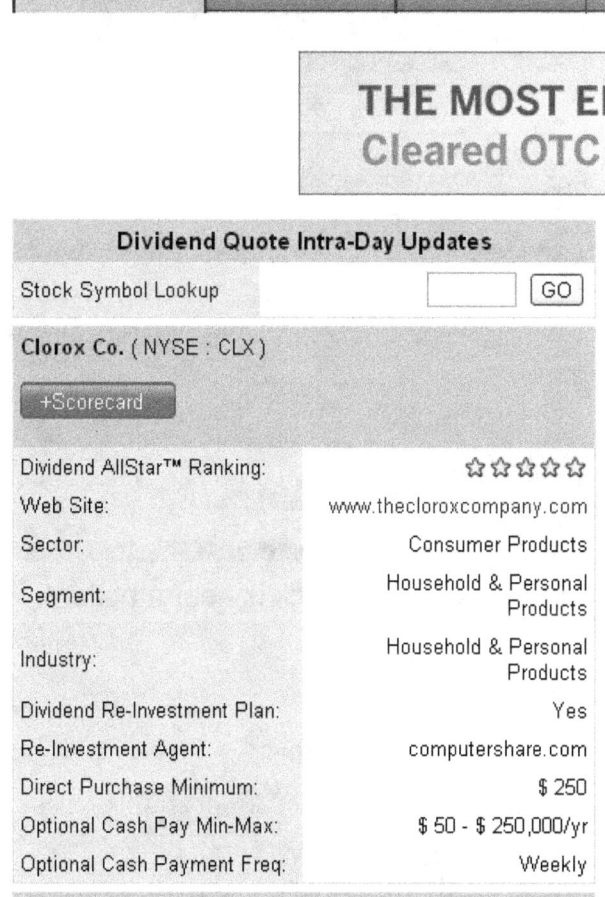

Some of the information is provided as a free service. If you are going to specialize in dividend paying stocks this service may be worth the monthly membership cost. Many online services can save you research time. Use the ones that relate to your style of investing.

Since most stocks track the general market direction there may be times when you can't find a good candidate. We are looking for stocks poised for an increase in price that pay dividends. When the market (SP-500) is near a top look for negative beta stocks to buy.

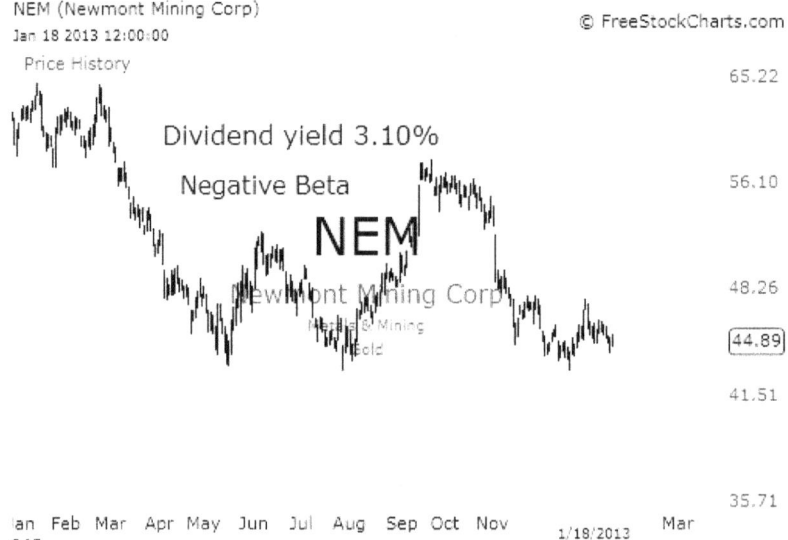

Pull up a chart to see if the stock is near a bottom.

Newmont Mining is a gold mining stock that is due for a price increase. Look up the dividend information to see if it will fit into your investment schedule. This stock should be increasing in price while most stocks are decreasing in price.

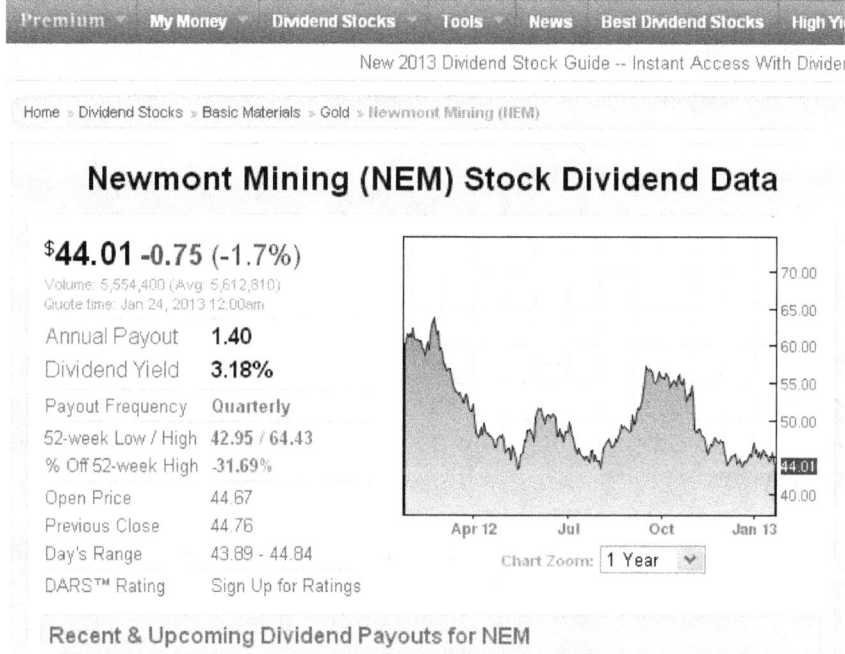

This is another good dividend service. Find the services that provide the best features for your needs.

Thinking is the hardest work there is, which is probably the reason why so few engage in it.
Henry Ford

If you are not interested in short term trading which can be considered weeks to months (in the context of this book). You can pull up longer time frame charts to get a view of the long term picture.

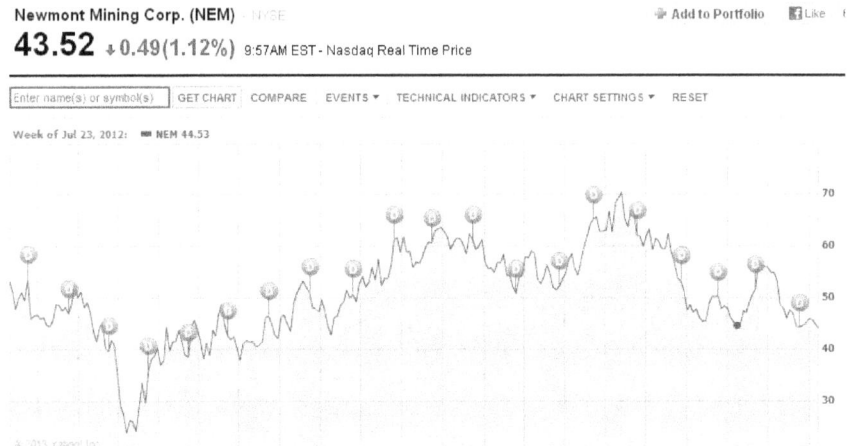

Newmont Mining Corp. (NEM) NYSE

43.52 ↓0.49(1.12%) 9:57AM EST - Nasdaq Real Time Price

Week of Jul 23, 2012: ▬ NEM 44.53

This is a five year chart from Yahoo Finance showing ex-dividend dates. I would say that this stock is on the low side of its price range. This may be a good time to buy and hold for a year.

The goal of this trade is collecting four dividend payments while profiting from the increased stock price. Whatever time frame we are trading, the rules remain the same. Buy when the stock price is low and sell when the stock price is high.

Dividend payments are icing on the cake.

Why trade for one or the other when you can have both. Even if your price chart analysis is wrong, the dividend payment will help to cut your loss. And you could hold the stock for as long as it takes to increase in price while collecting dividend payments.

To get a little more creative you can also sell covered calls on your dividend producing investment. This could be the cherry on the icing on the cake.

There are only a few optionable, dividend paying stocks. But it is a list of pretty good stocks.

Very Few Optionable Dividend Stocks

Symbol	Name	Industry	Last	Div	HisVol	Corr SPX
ETR	Entergy Corp	Utility – Electric Power	66.1	5.0%	11%	0.13
HR	Healthcare Realty	Reit – Equity Trust	22.97	5.4%	33%	0.03
MO	Altria Group	Tobacco	33.68	6.1%	18%	0.11
POM	Potomac Electric	Utility – Electric Power	19.37	5.6%	12%	-0.26
PPL	PPL Corp	Utility – Electric Power	27.73	5.2%	11%	-0.04
RAI	RJ Reynolds	Tobacco	42.49	5.4%	17%	-0.33

Big MO may not be poised for a good trade right now but maybe it will be when your ready to trade.

When you're ready to make this trade pull up an options chain and do a buy/write. A buy/write is buying a stock while at the same time selling a call.

The options do not pay a great deal of money because dividend paying stocks are not typically volatile. Volatility is a major component in option pricing.

1.82	1.86	2,288	32.00
1.20	1.22	5,179	33.00
			33.46
0.70	0.72	5,400	34.00
0.38	0.39	4,800	35.00
0.16	0.19	2,780	36.00

This trade will still add one or two percent to your bottom line. The buy/write trade is easy to initiate and usually requires a reduced commission rate.

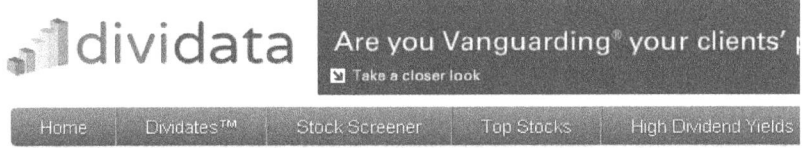

..ıll dividata   Are you Vanguarding® your clients'

☑ Take a closer look

| Home | Dividates™ | Stock Screener | Top Stocks | High Dividend Yields |

Top Rated Dividend Paying Stocks

What's the easiest way to find the highest rated stocks on Dividata? Just look at the list below! These stocks are sorted in descending order based on the size of their market capitalization (their total value in the stock market). Click on the stock symbol or company name for additional details on their dividend history, stock metrics, and fundamentals.

		Last Close	Dividend Yield	Years Paying	Dividata Rating
EMR	Emerson Electric Company	$56.87	2.88%	30	
BPL	Buckeye Partners L.P.	$54.51	7.61%	24	
RTN	Raytheon Company	$58.20	3.44%	31	
KDN	Kaydon Corporation	$24.41	3.28%	22	
GD	General Dynamics Corporation	$71.45	2.86%	33	
NOC	Northrop Grumman Corporation	$68.71	3.2%	30	
EEP	Enbridge Energy, L.P.	$30.30	7.19%	20	
LEG	Leggett & Platt, Incorporated	$29.24	3.97%	25	
UTL	UNITIL Corporation	$26.41	5.23%	20	
UVV	Universal Corporation	$53.40	3.75%	24	
DBD	Diebold, Incorporated	$32.66	3.49%	30	
MDP	Meredith Corporation	$34.32	4.46%	27	
CLX	Clorox Company (The)	$77.11	3.32%	29	
UTX	United Technologies Corporation	$88.07	2.43%	42	
MRK	Merck & Company, Inc.	$42.82	4.02%	42	
PAYX	Paychex, Inc.	$32.28	8.18%	22	
JNJ	Johnson & Johnson	$72.85	3.35%	42	
GIS	General Mills, Inc.	$41.51	3.18%	29	
NKE	Nike, Inc.	$53.09	3.16%	25	

Exchange Traded Funds also offer products that produce dividends. Some ETFs specialize in dividend paying securities.

Top Yielding ETFs — Page 1 of 6

Rank	ETF Name	ETF Symbol	ETF Category	Recent Yield
#1	KBW High Dividend Yield Financial Portfolio	KBWD	Income	8.33%
#2	CEF Income Composite Portfolio	PCEF	Value	7.48%
#3	SuperDividend ETF	SDIV	Income	7.38%
#4	iShares Global ex USD High Yield Corporate Bond Fund	HYXU		7.33%
#5	Guggenheim S&P Global Dividend Opportunities Index ETF	LVL	Income	7.17%
#6	iShares B - Ca Rated Corporate Bond Fund	QLTC		7.05%
#7	SPDR Barclays High Yield Bond ETF	JNK	Corporate Debt	6.70%
#8	SPDR Dow Jones International Real Estate ETF	RWX	Real Estate	6.57%
#9	iShares iBoxx $ High Yield Corporate Bond Fund	HYG	Corporate Debt	6.54%
#10	iShares FTSE EPRA/NAREIT Developed Asia Index Fund	IFAS	Asia	6.46%
#11	SPDR Wells Fargo Preferred Stock ETF	PSK	Income	6.36%
#12	First Trust STOXX European Select Dividend Index Fund	FDD	Europe	6.36%
#13	Preferred Portfolio	PGX	Income	6.33%
#14	Financial Preferred Portfolio	PGF	Income	6.19%
#15	SPDR S&P International Dividend ETF	DWX	Global	6.06%
#16	iShares Global High Yield Corporate Bond Fund	GHYG		6.03%
#17	iShares S&P U.S. Preferred Stock Index Fund	PFF	Income	6.02%
#18	iShares FTSE EPRA/NAREIT Developed Real Estate ex-U.S. Index Fund	IFGL	Real Estate	5.85%
#19	First Trust Dow Jones Global Select Dividend Index Fund	FGD	Income	5.73%
#20	Guggenheim ABC High Dividend ETF	ABCS	Income	5.38%
#21	KBW Premium Yield Equity REIT Portfolio	KBWY	Real Estate	5.35%
#22	SPDR S&P Emerging Markets Dividend ETF	EDIV	Emerging Markets	5.34%
#23	Guggenheim Multi-Asset Income ETF	CVY	Global	5.15%
#24	Guggenheim BulletShares 2015 High Yield Corporate Bond ETF	BSJF	Corporate Debt	5.09%
#25	SPDR S&P International Telecommunications Sector ETF	IST	Technology	4.95%
#26	High-Yield Municipal Index ETF	HYD	Municipal Bonds	4.95%
#27	iShares Dow Jones International Select Dividend Index Fund	IDV	Income	4.92%
#28	LatAm Aggregate Bond ETF	BONO	South America	4.85%
#29	Guggenheim BulletShares 2014 High Yield Corporate Bond ETF	BSJE	Corporate Debt	4.83%
#30	Low Volatility Emerging Markets Dividend ETF	HILO	Income	4.82%

The advantage to trading ETFs is the diversification of funds. Risk aversion tactics often rely on diversification of assets. Considering this aspect and the ability to trade optionable, dividend paying securities that trade like a stock............ what's not to like?

The secret of business is to know something that no one else knows.
Aristotle Onasis

Many online services provide the same kinds of information about dividend paying ETFs as for dividend paying stocks. All of the trading methods we have learned can be applied to ETFs.

Symbol	Name	Price	Change	Assets *	Avg. Vol	YTD
VIG	Vanguard Dividend Appreciation ETF	$63.19	+0.14%	$12,950,486	1,181,771	+6.08%
DVY	iShares Dow Jones Select Dividend Index Fund	$59.64	-0.05%	$10,816,438	1,228,280	+4.19%
SDY	SPDR S&P Dividend ETF	$61.50	+0.08%	$9,925,853	1,062,068	+5.73%
DEM	WisdomTree Emerging Markets High-Yielding Equity Fund	$57.10	-0.19%	$5,229,225	757,721	-0.16%
VYM	Vanguard High Dividend Yield Index Fund	$52.04	+0.29%	$4,627,523	653,434	+5.39%
HDV	iShares High Dividend Equity Fund	$61.57	+0.31%	$2,275,152	290,774	+4.77%
IDV	iShares Dow Jones EPAC Select Dividend Fund	$34.89	+0.66%	$1,604,579	373,829	+3.62%
DLN	WisdomTree World ex-U.S. Growth Fund	$56.05	+0.13%	$1,306,900	161,451	+4.47%
DGS	WisdomTree Emerging Markets SmallCap Dividend Fund	$49.82	-0.30%	$1,294,540	181,715	+0.77%
DWX	SPDR S&P International Dividend ETF	$49.18	+0.16%	$1,232,848	208,267	+2.33%
DTN	WisdomTree Dividend Top 100 Fund	$58.31	+0.24%	$1,053,245	203,602	+4.91%
PID	PowerShares International Dividend Achievers Portfolio	$16.47	-0.06%	$747,565	276,405	+4.04%
SCHD	US Dividend Equity ETF Profile	$29.95	+0.27%	$596,287	255,726	+5.68%
FVD	First Trust Value Line Dividend Fund	$18.08	-0.17%	$560,826	113,411	+4.51%
DHS	WisdomTree Equity Income Fund	$47.95	+0.08%	$553,668	89,624	+4.69%
FDL	First Trust Morningstar Dividend Leaders Index Fund	$19.11	-0.10%	$552,740	315,643	+3.52%
DLS	WisdomTree International SmallCap Dividend Fund	$54.38	+0.50%	$524,202	47,942	+4.32%
DES	WisdomTree SmallCap Dividend Fund	$53.53	+0.11%	$447,384	59,328	+4.99%
DWM	WisdomTree DEFA Fund	$48.21	+0.65%	$441,099	47,830	+3.74%
DON	WisdomTree MidCap Dividend Fund	$60.75	-0.08%	$424,270	53,414	+5.82%
EDIV	SPDR S&P Emerging Markets Dividend ETF	$47.05	-0.02%	$404,907	102,903	-0.28%
DOO	WisdomTree International Dividend ex-Financials Fund	$43.14	+0.65%	$354,078	36,910	+2.96%
PEY	PowerShares High Yield Equity Dividend Achievers Portfolio	$9.83	-0.10%	$287,328	156,219	+4.46%

When buying stocks and ETFs to collect dividends don't forget to consider the capital appreciation or depreciation due to a change in price. A price decrease could wipe out your dividend profits. Even long term investors can benefit from reading the charts.

I hope this book has been informative and useful. I have presented trading possibilities that are available to all investors. Further education is suggested. I wish you the best in your trading adventures

.

The hardest part of any journey is starting.
Dana DeCecco

84

An economist is an expert who will know
tomorrow why the things he predicted yesterday
didn't happen today.
Laurence J. Peter

Does this wave:

Look like this wave?

Hang zero, stop riding the waves !